KAPLAN pmbr

FINALS

FAMILY LAW

CORE CONCEPTS AND KEY QUESTIONS

Second Edition

T. Leigh Hearn, Esquire
Series Editor

© 2009 by Kaplan, Inc.

Published by Kaplan Publishing, a division of Kaplan, Inc.
1 Liberty Plaza, 24th floor
New York, NY 10006

Printed in the United States of America

10 9 8 7 6 5 4 3 2 1

ISBN13: 978-1-60714-098-6

TABLE OF CONTENTS

TABLE OF CONTENTS

I. BASIS FOR FAMILY LAW

A. SOURCES:

The law of the family is derived from several different sources.

1. **States:** Family law is generally not a national subject. Rather, each jurisdiction has its own common law and statutory law. However, there is some consistency among the states, and it is the consistencies that this outline covers.

2. **Federal Law:** While most family law is state specific, federal law applies in some situations, as in the case of a custody dispute between parents in different states or where a parent in another state from the child has not been paying child support.

3. **The United States Constitution:** The United States Constitution influences all of the basic rights of the family, including the right to marry, the right to procreate, the right to use contraception, the right to abortion, and the right of the family to make family-based decisions.

4. **Tax Law:** The tax code has a profound effect on the state of family law, because it may be beneficially or detrimental to people based on their marital or parental status.

5. **Local Regulations:** Various states and communities have passed ordinances defining "family" in different ways, especially in the area of long-term same-sex or opposite-sex couples.

6. **International Law:** Recently, international law has played a major role in the area of family law, particularly in the area of adoption, immigration (where a citizen of a foreign country wishes to marry a United States citizen), and in the area of foreign divorces.

II. MARRIAGE

A. DUAL STATUS OF MARRIAGE

1. **Marriage as Religious Event:** Marriage has a long history as a religious ceremony in many traditions. In particular, the Judeo-Christian tradition affected the English common law through the ecclesiastical (church) courts and laws which had jurisdiction over the marital state until the 1800s.

2. **Marriage as Civil Event:** Marriage now has a distinct civil/legal status. The requirements for marriage are set forth in state statutes and decisions of the civil courts. Marriage is contractual in nature with certain mandatory conditions and other aspects that may be circumvented by the agreement of the

parties, e.g., postnuptial agreements, antenuptial agreements (also known as prenuptial or premarital agreements) (antenuptial and prenuptial agreements).

EXAMPLE: Christy, whose religion does not sanction divorce, is married to Don. While her church may not recognize her divorce, all American states do recognize divorce and Christy may be legally, although not necessarily religiously, divorced from Don.

B. **DEFINITION: Marriage, at least from a civil perspective, is defined and controlled by state law presumed.**

1. **Challenges to Conventional Definition — One Man and One Woman:** Until recently, all states simply presumed marriage to be a union between one man and one woman. In response to certain movements in favor of the adoption of same-sex marriage, federal legislation known as the Defense of Marriage Act (DOMA) was enacted in 1996. DOMA makes clear that no state under the full faith and credit clause of the constitution will be required to recognize a marriage entered into by persons of the same sex even though such marriage may be valid in another state. In addition, the act also states that the federal government will not recognize such unions as marriages and therefore the parties to such a partnership will not receive the same benefits and status as that of a marriage between one man and one woman. In 2003, Massachusetts became the first state to recognize a right, grounded in the state constitution, for same sex couples to marry. Other states have enacted legislation defining marriage as a civil union between one man and one woman. For example, in November of 2008, voters in California and Florida voted to amend their state constitutions to explicitly define marriage as between one man and one woman.

2. **Bigamy:** It is illegal for anyone to be married to more than one person at any one time. The justifications for this limitation have varied over time, but this rule has invariably been upheld.

   a. **Criminal Implications of Bigamy:** Failure to abide by this rule will render subsequent marriages void and may subject someone who intentionally violates the rule to criminal prosecution for bigamy (or, less frequently, criminal adultery).

   b. **Civil Implications of Bigamy:** Although the marriage is void, in most states the children will still be deemed to be legitimate. Further, if one of the spouses is an innocent victim, he or she may be entitled to alimony, and, under certain circumstances, the marriage may either become valid as a common law marriage or become a valid marriage under a savings statute.

   EXAMPLE: Charles White is married to Cynthia. Charles and Cynthia both are members of a religion that recognizes and honors the practice of polygamy. Therefore, Charles marries a second wife, Anna. In most states, Charles may be prosecuted for violating anti-bigamy laws, even though his bigamy is supported by and sanctioned by his church.

C. VALIDITY

1. **In General:** In general, the validity of a marriage is determined by the state or foreign country where the marriage was celebrated.

2. **Recognition of Marriage:** Marriages valid in the state or foreign country where the marriage occurred will usually be recognized as valid elsewhere unless such recognition would violate fundamental public policy. Such recognition follows from the comity granted by and between states and countries. This issue has become particularly acute with the recent controversy over "same sex" marriages, the status of which has been subject to litigation and statutory enactment. As previously mentioned DOMA specifies that states are not required to give effect to same sex marriages of other states.

D. NATURE OF RIGHTS AND OBLIGATIONS

1. **Constitutional Dimension:** The United States Supreme Court has found that a variety of aspects of marriage have constitutional implications. Thus, the right to marry is subject to equal protection analysis and may not be restricted on the basis of race. Other decisions have raised issues of due process constitutional privacy, and free exercise of religion.

2. **Common Law:** Common law treated the marriage as creating a single person— the husband. All property and decision-making resided with the husband; the wife had little legal status.

3. **Modification by Statute:** Common law was modified over time by statute to grant rights to women. Wives were given the right to own and convey property, to enter into binding contracts, and other rights previously only granted to men.

4. **Retroactive Effect:** Typically, laws may not be applied retroactively. Modifications of the rights and obligations of the marital state may affect existing marriages. Although such modifications may appear to have a retroactive effect since the marriage was solemnized before the modification, challenges based on such retroactive effect have uniformly failed.

5. **Modification by Agreement:** The parties to a marriage may modify their obligations during and after marriage by agreements variously called prenuptial, premarital, antenuptial, or postnuptial agreements. Such agreements usually address financial issues in the event of death or divorce, such as property distribution and support obligations.

   a. **Validity:** In general, such agreements will be governed by the state law of contract, including doctrines such as duress and fraud, and application of the constraints of public policy. Thus, an agreement that is deemed to be patently oppressive or unfair will not be enforced. Further, such agreements may not override the fundamental rights of the parties (such as the right to seek divorce or to own property).

b. **Requirements:** Most states require prenuptial agreements to be in writing under their Statute of Frauds or other special statute. As usual, these requirements may be waived under certain conditions such as reliance, partial performance, fraud on the part of the invoking party, and the like. In the absence of statutory provisions, prenuptial agreements must be supported by adequate consideration, although the mutual promises to marry will generally satisfy this requirement. States that have enacted the Uniform Premarital Agreement Act ("UPAA") or the Uniform Marital Property Act ("UPMA") no longer require consideration.

E. BREACH OF OR INTERFERENCE WITH PROMISE TO MARRY

1. **Existence of Action for Breach of Promise:** Although not widely recognized, a few states still recognize actions for breach of the promise to marry or interference with such promise. These actions, traditionally known as "heartbalm actions," arise in tort rather than contract. As a result, damages are generally limited to remedial rather than expectation damages, although some states permit recovery of expected benefits or of injury to feelings, health, and reputation.

   a. **Requirements:** To prevail, the plaintiff must prove the existence of an actual promise to marry. In the absence of a public, formal engagement, such promise may be demonstrated by circumstantial evidence including the exchange of rings, public declaration, and joint preparation for wedding.

2. **Existence of Action for Interference:** Historically called "alienation of affection," this tort is analogous to the tort of interference with contractual relations. In principle, it allows a spouse or putative spouse to recover for conduct that causes a partner to transfer his or her affections to another person, whether or not that person was the defendant. In modern practice, this action has all but disappeared.

F. GIFTS IN CONTEMPLATION OF MARRIAGE: It is not unusual for one person to give another a gift that is premised on the future marriage. The most typical example is the engagement ring itself, inherently a symbol of the planned marriage. Gifts can also include rights in real estate, trust property, or other items of value. If the gift is specifically given in anticipation of marriage, then it is considered a conditional gift and is returnable if the event does not occur. The majority of states consider fault in breaking the engagement to be irrelevant. If on the other hand, the gift is given for another reason—such as a Christmas present—or simply as an expression of affection, the gift is not returnable. The same analysis applies to gifts by third parties to the engaged couple; if given in anticipation of a marriage that does not occur, the gift is returnable. The basis for the gift is a factual matter of proof.

G. TYPES OF MARRIAGE: There are two types of marriage, formal or statutory marriage and common law marriage. All states have a process for couples to comply

with certain procedures to complete a marriage ceremony – often called the "solemnization" of the marriage. Some states also have acknowledged a marriage called "common law marriage" that allows the couple to achieve the marital state without complying with the requirement for a formal marriage.

H. MANDATORY REQUIREMENTS FOR ALL MARRIAGES

1. **Consent:** In order for a marriage to be valid, both parties must give voluntary and valid consent.

   a. **Voluntary:** Contrary to the stories of "shotgun" marriages, no marriage is valid if either spouse is acting under duress. Consent must be given voluntarily. This also precludes marriage procured by fraud or deceit.

   b. **Valid Consent:** In order for consent to be valid, the person must be competent to give consent. Thus, he or she must be competent to understand the nature of the action and the implications of the decision to marry. Evaluation of competence does not include, however, whether marriage is a good decision. Thus, a person who is mentally disabled may still have the ability to enter into a valid marriage if he or she is deemed to satisfy this requirement. On the other hand, a person of normal capacity may not be meet this requirement if sufficiently impaired by drugs or alcohol or some other temporary impairment.

   c. **Substitute Consent:** In some circumstances, a person otherwise deemed not competent may be permitted to marry with the consent of a legal guardian.

2. **Intent:** Each of the parties must have the intent to marry. Thus, a sham marriage, or a marriage entered into in jest or for fraudulent purposes will not be valid.

3. **Consanguinity:** No marriage of any type will be valid if it violates the state's rules on consanguinity—closeness of relationship. Some degrees of relationship violate every state's laws such as brother/sister or parent/child. With relatively few exceptions, uncle/niece, aunt/nephew marriages are inherently prohibited. Approximately one half of states prohibit first cousins from marrying.

   a. **Step and Adoptive Relationships:** Although the genetic argument against step and adoptive relationships is not effective, most states still apply consanguinity rules even if the relationship arises from adoption or a step relationship. On occasion, such rules have been challenged, but in general, they are still valid.

4. **Age:** Regardless of other factors, every state has established a minimum age for marriage. That age varies from state to state. Many states also establish a secondary age limit that will permit marriage if parental consent is obtained. Some states also permit a court order in lieu of parental consent. Historically, some states set different age limits for men and women; there is a general consensus now that such distinctions are impermissible.

a. **Implications of Age Violation:** Unlike consanguinity violations, which almost invariably mean that the marriage is void, violations of age limits may either be void or voidable depending on state law. Further, age violations can be curable.

I. **STATUTORY MARRIAGE:** In order to complete a statutory marriage, the couple must comply with each of the requirements of the state in which the marriage takes place. Such requirements vary, but generally include the following.

1. **Marriage License:** Although denominated a "license," this documentation is routinely available to any person who meets the state requirements for marriage. Its purpose is to formally recognize that no legal impediments to the marriage exist, rather than establishing any independent requirements. It serves more to document that no impediments exist rather than establishing any independent requirements.

   CAVEAT: In some situations a license is not necessarily required. For example, where a couple is married in a church without a license, the courts have held that, in the absence of a statute expressly making a marriage invalid without a license, where a long-term marriage results, such a marriage is valid even without the license having been obtained at the beginning of marriage. This is particularly true where one "spouse" had a good faith belief that the couple possessed a valid license.

2. **Blood Test:** Many states require that each partner be tested for certain diseases, principally syphilis or other venereal diseases. However, even if one partner tests positive for such diseases, he or she may typically marry if his or her partner grants informed consent.

3. **Waiting Period/Expiration Period:** Most states, but not all, impose a minimum waiting period before the issuance of a marriage license or before the marriage license becomes valid. Imposed to avoid impulsive marriages, the waiting period is typically very short (and, indeed long waiting periods might well be considered unconstitutional because they would constitute an undue burden on the fundamental right to marry). Some states waive the waiting period upon completion of a premarital counseling course offered by the state. Marriage licenses have extended periods of validity, but will eventually expire.

4. **Ceremony:** Statutory marriages must be solemnized by an authorized person. In general, states give such power to clergy, judges, notary publics, and certain civil officials such as justices of the peace or others. Some states also issue one-time licenses to citizens to perform the ceremony. The person solemnizing the marriage is required to complete and file the license with the appropriate agency.

5. **Failure to Comply with Statutory Requirements:** In the absence of fraud, most states will recognize the validity of a marriage that was intended to comply with statutory requirements but failed to do so. Thus, a couple formally married in church but without a license who then acted as man and wife were deemed married. Similarly, a marriage performed by a person not qualified to do so will often be recognized, particularly if at least one of the parties was unaware of this status.

6. **Putative Marriage.**

   a. **Definition:** A putative marriage may exist where one person has been living with a member of the opposite sex in a genuine belief that the two are married, even though they are not. Such a marriage may arise where, *ab initio* (at the outset), there was some legal impediment to the marriage—for example, a previous marriage, a previously unknown blood relationship, or some other impediment—of which the innocent spouse was unaware. Such a relationship is not a valid marriage and is not enforceable as one.

   b. **Rights of Innocent Spouse:** However, because the innocent party had a good faith belief that s/he was married, s/he may be entitled to compensation and/or benefits upon discovery of the defect and termination of the relationship, just as s/he would be in the case of a divorce in a legitimate marriage.

7. **Special Statutory Marriages:** Some states have special provisions to cover unusual situations. For example, if one party is prevented from attending the ceremony itself as a result of military service, a few states will permit a proxy marriage when a third person acts in place of the absent partner. Another special situation arises in states which do not recognize common law marriage that permits persons holding themselves out as a married couple who are permitted to have a confidential marriage ceremony to formalize their relationship. It is important to note that not all special marriages will be recognized as valid by other states or the federal government.

J. **COMMON LAW MARRIAGE:** Although only recognized by a handful of states, there still exists an alternative form of marriage called common law marriage. In essence, if the participants comply with the state's requirements, they may be deemed married even if they do not complete a statutory marriage. In general, common law marriages will be recognized even in states that do not permit it under the general principles of comity and the policies in favor or recognition of marriages. The requirements vary from state to state, but generally include the following:

1. **Cohabitation:** In general, the partners must live together as a married couple.

2. **Present Agreement:** The parties must agree to enter a common law marriage.

3. **Holding Out:** The parties must hold themselves out as man and wife. Merely living together is not enough; the parties must generally inform friends, relatives, and the community—that they are, in fact, married. Historically, the use of a common surname was a significant indication, but that has become less important as married couples frequently use different surnames. Holding joint property, common bank accounts, and joint tax returns are other typical indicia.

   NOTE: Contrary to common belief, no set period of time for cohabitation is required in most jurisdictions.

NOTE: Where "spouses" live together and hold themselves out to be husband and wife, but are not actually married because of some impediment to the marriage (such as a prior existing marriage) where the impediment is removed (e.g., the former marriage is dissolved) a valid common law marriage may result if there has been a marriage ceremony.

K. **IMPLICATIONS OF MARRIAGE:** There are a variety of legal consequences of marriage, some are benefits and some are obligations.

1. **Real Property:** Most states create a special way of holding property that only applies to married couples. This is termed tenancy by the entirety, which allows for the surviving spouse to take ownership of the property without passage through an estate.

2. **General Property Rights:** Most states are "separate property" states. A few, most notably California, are "community property" states.

   a. **Separate Property:** In these states, each spouse may acquire and maintain sole ownership of property, whether or not the property was brought to the marriage or acquired during the marriage. This does not mean that, in the event of divorce, a court may not use its equitable powers to re-allocate the property; it only means that there is no presumption applied concerning the ownership of the property. "Separate property" states do not preclude joint ownership of property, and many couples maintain joint accounts and the like.

   b. **Community Property:** While the details of community property vary from state to state, the general principle is that property acquired during the marriage is under the joint control and ownership of each spouse and must be allocated by the courts in accordance with that principle, regardless of which spouse caused the property to come to the marriage.

3. **Rights of Support:** Some states still impose obligations of one spouse to support the other. Historically imposed on the husband, the doctrine has been modified to be applicable to either spouse.

4. **Marital Privilege:** To protect the privacy of marriage, many states permit a spouse to refuse to testify against the other spouse about private communications made in the context of the marriage.

5. **Name:** Traditionally, the wife changed her last name to match that of her husband. This was not required, it was simply a custom. Similarly, children of the marriage took the husband's surname as well. In the modern era, it has become more common for the wife to keep her name and not unknown for the couple to take on a new joint name, either a hyphenated version of their two names, or a third name entirely.

III. CIVIL UNION/DOMESTIC PARTNERSHIP

A. **DEFINITION:** A civil union or a domestic partnership is a marriage-like relationship between two people of the same sex. Since 2000, when Vermont became the first state to statutorily approve civil unions, several states have enacted statutes to permit same sex couples to enter into civil unions or domestic partnerships.

B. **REQUIREMENTS**

1. **License and Ceremony:** The requirements for entry into a civil union or domestic partnership are almost identical to those for a marriage in most states. Couples must obtain a state-issued license and must participate in a ceremony at which a state-approved officiant presides.

2. **Other Requirements:** As in a heterosexual marriage, in order to enter into a civil union or domestic partnership, the partners must demonstrate that they are not closely related by blood, that they both enter into the union willingly, and that they are not committed by marriage or civil union to any other relationship.

C. **STATUS:** The parties to a civil union or domestic partnership are generally entitled to similar benefits and obligations as are spouses in a heterosexual marriage.

D. **RECOGNITION BY OTHER JURISDICTIONS:** Despite principles of comity, many other jurisdictions do not recognize civil unions or domestic partnerships because, in their opinion, there is a strong public policy reason against doing so.

E. **DISSOLUTION:** Should the parties to a civil union or domestic partnership wish to end the relationship, they must do so formally according to the rules of the issuing state.

F. **RIGHTS OF THE PARTIES UPON DISSOLUTION:** The parties may agree to or petition for alimony, support, and property division, just as would the spouses in a heterosexual marriage. Similarly, if the couple has children, the court will use a traditional analysis in awarding custody and child support.

IV. ANNULMENT

A. **DEFINITION:** Annulment is a declaration that a prior marriage was void *ab initio* and was ineffective. As a result, the two partners were never married.

B. **DUAL STATUS OF ANNULMENT**

1. **Annulment as a Religious Event:** Some religions, notably the Roman Catholic church, still have prohibitions on divorce and remarriage. As a result, it is essential for those who adhere to such beliefs to obtain an adjudication of annulment of the religious aspect of their marriage.

2. **Annulment as a Civil Event:** Annulment can also be obtained from a civil court. The distinctions between civil annulment and divorce have somewhat diminished as courts more frequently impose obligations of support even in annulment situations.

C. **GROUNDS FOR ANNULMENT:** In general, the grounds for annulment include all those grounds that would render a marriage either void or voidable. If the basis is that the marriage is void, the court's action is simply formal acknowledgment of the legal absence of marriage. If it is an impediment that renders the marriage voidable, then the court's action constitutes the election of one or both of the partners to declare the marriage a nullity.

1. **Fraud:** In order for a marriage to be annulled because of fraud, the fraudulent misrepresentation must (i) have taken place before the marriage event, (ii) be material and go to the "essence of the marriage," and (iii) have been relied on by the defrauded party. The issue of materiality/"essence of the marriage" is a fact question but may include questions of fertility, religious intention or status, pregnancy, or paternity. On the other hand, issues of wealth, character, and history, even if misrepresented, will not be the basis for an annulment.

[handwritten: elements of fraud]

2. **Sham or Jest:** Marriages that are entered into without the serious intent to marry are not true marriages. As a result, the court's declaration of annulment is simply the recognition of the true status of the marriage. Similarly, a sham marriage in which both parties understand that the marriage was intended to be ineffective also fails to satisfy the requirement that the parties have the true intention to be married. If, on the other hand, one of the parties truly intended to be married, then the court may determine that, as to that spouse, the marriage may be deemed valid.

3. **Duress:** A marriage in which one or both partners act under duress also lacks the true consent necessary for a valid marriage. In order to demonstrate duress, the party seeking the annulment must demonstrate that the duress occurred before the marriage and was sufficiently severe to constrain that party's free will. The test is a subjective test that focuses on the party at issue rather than a reasonable person. Typically, physical force, threat of arrest or prosecution (except for certain crimes such as seduction), and blackmail have been deemed sufficient.

D. **VOID VS. VOIDABLE MARRAIGES:** Both void and voidable marriages may be annulled. However, there is an important legal difference between the two.

1. **Void Marriages:** A void marriage is one against which there is strong public policy. Both bigamous and incestuous marriages are void *ab initio*, meaning that no annulment is necessary to end them. However, some people choose to annul void marriages because they want a legal document declaring that the marriage is over.

   NOTE: If a marriage is void *ab initio*, the parties never had legal married status even if they obtained a license and observed other marital formalities.

2. **Voidable Marriages:** A voidable marriage may also be annulled. Such a marriage arises when one party has not been fully honest with the other at the time of the marriage (such as about ability or intention to have sexual relations or children after the marriage, or other such concerns that are material to the marriage), or when one party married the other under duress.

   a. **Ratification:** The parties to a voidable marriage may "ratify" the marriage if they wish, meaning that they may decide that the concern that made the marriage voidable is no longer an issue. For example, if one party initially married under duress, s/he may declare that s/he now freely decides to marry the same spouse. Continuing to cohabitate after discovery of a material defect in the marriage may also ratify the marriage. Once a marriage has been ratified, it is no longer voidable, and therefore it will not qualify for annulment.

3. **Survival of One Spouse after the Death of Another:** In the case of a void marriage, where one "spouse" survives the other, that "spouse" is not considered to be such in most states. Therefore, the spouse does not qualify for intestate succession. However, where a marriage is voidable, the opposite is true. A voidable marriage is considered to be a valid marriage until and unless an annulment is obtained. Therefore, the surviving spouse would be entitled to inherit through intestate succession.

E. **DEFENSES TO ANNULMENT:** A party seeking to defeat annulment of a voidable marriage can invoke the usual equitable defenses to a legal action. Thus, ratification, estoppel, or unclean hands can be invoked to forestall such an action. Such defenses cannot be used in an action arising from a marriage that is inherently void; the annulment action simply recognizes its lack of validity. Nonetheless, a party to a marriage deemed void who has acted unfairly or fraudulently may not unfairly assert such invalidity to his or her unfair advantage.

F. **IMPLICATIONS OF ANNULMENT**

1. **Children:** Children of an annulled marriage are still deemed to be legitimate. Furthermore, the presumption of paternity will also not be disturbed.

2. **Financial Implications:** Although an annulment in principle declares that the marriage has never taken place, courts still have the power to declare the financial rights and obligations of the parties. Thus, the court may award alimony, child support, or a division of property. Under certain circumstances, the effect of an annulment may revive a prior spouse's support obligations.

G. **JURISDICTION:** There are two types of jurisdictional questions that arise. First, whether the state can impose limits on the availability of divorce. Second, whether a state has the power to issue a divorce decree that is effective against a spouse who is not present.

1. **Limits on Access:** Most states impose a residency requirement before allowing access to the courts for a divorce. These requirements have been found to be constitutionally permissible.

2. **Jurisdiction to Issue a Decree:** Clearly, if both parties are before the court, there is no impediment to the issuance of a decree. If only one of the partners is before the court, the court will still have jurisdiction to issue the divorce decree that will be effective and recognized by other states as to the termination of the marriage. Adjudications as to alimony, child support, and property allocation may not be recognized in the absence of personal jurisdiction, but that jurisdiction, as with other types of cases, may be established by long arm statutes if the requirements of the state statute are satisfied and the exercise of jurisdiction is consistent with minimum standards of constitutional due process.

   a. **End the Marriage – Subject Matter Jurisdiction:** In granting a divorce there is a distinction between the issuance of a divorce decree terminating the marriage and a divorce decree that has financial implications such as property division and/or support obligations in the form of child support or alimony. In order for a court to issue a divorce decree that effectuates only the termination of the marriage, a court only needs subject matter jurisdiction over the action as the court is not required to have personal jurisdiction over both litigants because the court will not be imposing regulation and requirements on the absent party. This subject matter jurisdiction is usually fulfilled by a standard residency requirement. For instance, the filing party must have resided in the selected forum state for a defined statutory period before a court in the forum will hear such action.

   b. **End the Marriage and Divide Property and Define Support Obligations:** In order to grant such a decree the court must have not only subject matter jurisdiction over the action but personal jurisdiction over both parties to the action as well. Of course, the filing party automatically consents to the personal jurisdiction of the selected forum by filing such an action. In order to ensure the court has personal jurisdiction over the responding party to such action the court will look to the long arm statute of the selected forum if the other non filing spouse does not live within the state.

   c. **Special Federal Legislation Dealing with Jurisdiction:**

      i. **Child Custody (UCCJEA):** Jurisdiction in child custody cases is governed by the Uniform Child Custody Jurisdiction and Enforcement Act (hereinafter "UCCJEA"). In Child Custody actions personal jurisdiction over both parties to the action is not required. The UCCJEA governs jurisdictional conflicts between states when parents reside in different states. The UCCJEA is intended to ensure that custody decisions are made in the state having the closest connection to the child and parents. It is also intended to discourage parental kidnapping and forum shopping and to facilitate enforcement of custody orders between states. In determining original jurisdiction the first inquiry is to determine whether a child has a "home state." The "home state" is defined as the place of residence where the child has resided six months consecutively prior to the filing of an action involving a custody dispute. This provision deters kidnapping and forum shopping as even if one parent moves with a child to another forum, the prior state still has exclusive jurisdiction over the proceeding until the moving parent has established residence for a term of six months in the new forum. In addition, UCCJEA provides that once a court has established original jurisdiction that court retains continuing jurisdiction over all modification proceedings so long as the original state remains the residence of the child or any party to the original proceeding.

ii. **SUPPORT (UIFSA):** The Uniform Interstate Family Support Act governs jurisdiction as it pertains to support when the parties to an action live in different states. Unlike UCCJEA, UIFSA requires personal jurisdiction. UIFSA extends a state's long arm statute to provide additional avenues to exercise personal jurisdiction over a party. If the long arm provisions are unsuccessful, the litigation must be brought in the state where the payor resides.

V. DIVORCE

A. **DEFINITION:** Divorce is the legal termination of the marital state. There are two types of divorces, fault based divorces (i.e. a divorce based on one partner's failure to abide by certain rules of conduct for married persons) and "no-fault" divorces, which may be obtained when one or both parties cease to desire to continue the marriage.

1. **Religious Implications of Civil Divorce:** Although legal divorce is effective for all civil purposes, it may not be effective in some religious contexts because of the dual nature of marriage. For example, Orthodox Jews may still need to get the religious equivalent of a divorce—a "get"—under the rules of the religious court.

B. **BASIS FOR DIVORCE:** Although no state still relies exclusively on fault-based divorce, it is preserved in a large number of states. In some states, a fault-based divorce may have either no waiting period or a lesser waiting period and may also have an impact on alimony and property rights. Further, since child custody is generally based on the best interests of the child, as discussed below, a finding of fault may also have implications for an award of custody.

1. **Fault Divorces:** Divorces based on fault require a finding that one spouse has violated one of the basic rules for marriage.

   a. **Adultery:** One of the traditional bases for a fault divorce arises when one partner engages in sexual relations with a person other than his or her spouse.

b. **Physical or Mental Cruelty:** The precise level or type of cruelty involved is a fact-based determination, but generally involves either a continuing pattern of conduct or a limited series—or even a single event—of extreme conduct.

c. **Desertion:** Mere absence does not constitute desertion. To meet this requirement, the parties cannot have agreed that the absent party will live elsewhere, the absent party must not have the intent to return, and the absence must not be provoked by the other spouse. Some states impose a minimum period for the continuous absence of one of the parties. A few courts have created the doctrine of "constructive desertion" when one party engages in intolerable conduct that causes the other to leave the marital home.

d. **Certain Health Issues:** In some states, insanity, impotence, contraction of a permanent disease, or addiction to alcohol or drugs may be the basis for a fault-based divorce.

2. **Defenses to Fault Divorce:** Because a fault divorce imposes adverse implications on the defending party, the state law typically permits such party to "defend" the action. Such defense may not preclude the divorce—since the court may, in any event, declare a no-fault divorce—but may avoid the results of a finding of fault.

a. **Collusion:** Collusion is rarely invoked as a defense because, by definition, it involves both spouses agreeing to obtain a fault divorce under false pretenses. More common when no-fault divorce was unavailable, it still occasionally arises. Should the court or an intervenor—such as a guardian ad litem—invoke and prove collusion, it will preclude a fault-based divorce and may also cause further sanctions for fraud in the judicial process.

b. **Provocation/Recrimination/Connivance:** Three closely related doctrines are provocation, recrimination, and connivance. Each of them vitiates the fault implications of the conduct at issue. Recrimination arises when both spouses are at fault (within the meaning of the divorce context); in this case, neither is entitled to a fault-based divorce. Some states require that the offenses be of approximately the same magnitude; others do not. Provocation arises when one spouse causes the other to commit the offense. For example, if one spouse provides drugs to the other and addiction results, then fault will not apply. Connivance occurs when one spouse creates the opportunity for the other to commit the offense on which the fault divorce is based. Thus, if one spouse facilitates an act of infidelity, fault divorce cannot be based on that act.

c. **Condonation:** If the innocent spouse forgives the offending spouse, it is the equivalent of a waiver of the grounds for a fault divorce. Forgiveness may be explicit or implied by the circumstances.

3. **No-Fault Divorce**

   a. **Definition:** As its name suggests, no-fault divorce permits the termination of a marriage without the finding that either party has violated one of the rules that are the grounds for a fault-based divorce.

   b. **Requirements:** Typically, states require only that the marriage be demonstrated to be irretrievably broken, or, put another way, that the partners are no longer compatible. Regardless of the way the state phrases the issue, the functional termination of the marriage is usually established by affidavit. Some states also permit a no-fault divorce to be based on actual separation for a period of time, the length varying by state. Some states permit the foundational separation to be purely by agreement of the parties; others require that it be established by court order.

4. **Separation:** Some states recognize the intermediate step between marriage and divorce, which is legal separation. A court-ordered separation order may arrange financial issues and child custody very similar to a divorce. The parties are still married, however, and may not remarry. Such an intermediate stage still preserves the possibility of reconciliation. Should the parties choose to proceed, however, to a full divorce, it can be done relatively quickly. Frequently, the financial and custody arrangements are simply continued into the divorce.

C. FINANCIAL IMPLICATIONS OF DIVORCE

1. **Property Division**

   a. **Definition of "Property":** In dividing property the court will divide both assets and liabilities. While tangible personal and real property obviously fall under the definition of the property that will be divided in a divorce, states have expanded the concept of property to include, for example, personal injury awards, pension benefits, workman's compensation benefits, Social Security income, interests in pending lawsuits, and interests in the other spouse's professional degree or license.

   b. **Non-Marital Property:** Assets and liabilities acquired prior to the marriage are considered that spouse's non-marital property. Also, some property acquired during the marriage can also be considered a spouse's non-marital property. Each state will define which property can be acquired during a marriage yet considered non-marital. Some examples include inheritances and monies from a personal injury lawsuit. Unless certain actions are taken by either spouse to change the title or the value of the property during the marriage, that property remains the sole and separate property of the spouse upon divorce.

c. **Converting Non-Marital Property to Marital Property:** Property or assets held by each spouse prior to the marriage or obtained during the marriage in one of the "non-marital" categories can remain the separate property of each spouse so long as no actions are taken that might convert the property or portion of the value of the property into a marital asset.

   i. **Transmutation by Title:** This entails changing the title holder of the property from one spouse's name to joint names, implying a "gift" was made to the marriage. An examples would be real property. Under these circumstances, the entire value of the property is considered "marital."

   ii. **Transmutation by Commingling:** This deals with commingling, or combining marital and nonmarital assets so that the value of each is virtually indistinguishable). An example might be a bank account containing pre-marital funds, where marital income is deposited and funds are withdrawn. Like transmutation by title, commingling converts the entire asset into "marital" property.

   iii. **Enhancement/Appreciation:** This involves converting a portion of the value of a non-marital asset into a marital asset, when the value of a non-marital asset is enhanced or appreciates in value due to the labor or financial contribution of either spouse during the marriage. When faced with an asset whose value has enhanced or appreciated as a direct result of either party's marital labor or funds, only the enhanced value is a marital asset. The value of the property as of the date of marriage remains non-marital. One example would be a real estate investment: if marital funds or labor paid down the mortgage or improved the property, the increase in value to the property attributable to those acts are marital.

d. **Marital Property:** Marital property is generally defined as property acquired during the marriage with marital funds or labor, regardless of whose name the property is titled under. If assets are acquired during a marriage with marital income or funds those assets are marital.

   i. **Treatment of Marital Property During Marriage:** States differ on how spouses can treat property during the marriage.

   (a) **Separate Property:** Most states use this approach. Under a separate property regime, how property is titled controls which spouse has the right to manage and control, including dispose of, property titled in his or her name, whether the property is marital or non-marital, as that distinction arises during divorce, not during the intact marriage.

   (b) **Community Property:** Under a community property regime, whether property is marital or non-marital is an important distinction during the marriage. Unlike states that permit title to control, community property states give each spouse equal say in the management and control, including disposition, of any marital property, during the marriage.

ii. **Treatment of Marital Property Upon Divorce:**

(a) **In a Divorce,** the assets and liabilities comprising the marital estate must be divided. First, all assets and liabilities must be identified. Second, all assets and liabilities must be classified as marital or non-marital, so that the non-marital property can be set aside to that party before the marital estate is divided. Third, each component of the marital estate must be valued. Fourth, each component of the marital estate must be distributed to one of the parties.

(b) **Equal Distribution:** Some states automatically divide all marital property equally between the parties.

(c) **Equitable Distribution:** Most states presume that the property will be divided equally, but allow for the marital estate to be divided unequally, as long as the result is equitable. The court will examine several factors, which may include the following:

  (i) the contribution to the marriage by each spouse, including contributions to the care and education of the children and services as homemaker.
  (ii) The economic circumstances of the parties.
  (iii) The duration of the marriage.
  (iv) Any interruption of personal careers or educational opportunities of either party.
  (v) The contribution of one spouse to the personal career or educational opportunity of the other spouse.
  (vi) The desirability of retaining any asset, including an interest in a business, corporation, or professional practice, intact and free from any claim or interference by the other party.
  (vii) The contribution of each spouse to the acquisition, enhancement, and production of income or the improvement of, or the incurring of liabilities to, both the marital assets and the nonmarital assets of the parties.
  (viii) The desirability of retaining the marital home as a residence for any dependent child of the marriage.
  (ix) The intentional dissipation, waste, depletion, or destruction of marital assets during the marriage.

e. **Effect of Fault:** Even in states that preserve fault-based divorces, fault has little to do with property division. However, some states do consider fault, also called marital misconduct, and will evaluate whether one spouse intentionally dissipated marital assets, by, for example, spending marital funds on an extramarital affair. When dividing the remaining marital estate, the spouse who was wrongfully deprived of the value of the asset such asset may given a greater distribution of the remaining property or assets as compensation for such dissipation.

f. Unlike child custody, alimony, and child support, the division of marital assets and liabilities is final and cannot be modified in a subsequent action due to a change in circumstances.

2. **Alimony:** Although alimony—also called "maintenance"—was traditionally awarded to the wife based on the husband's obligation of support, that limitation has been found to be constitutionally defective. Now, to the extent alimony is considered by the court, it is a mutual obligation. An award of alimony is based on one spouse's need for alimony and the other spouse's ability to pay.

Types of Alimony

1. Temporary alimony or alimony *pendente lite*—Alimony granted on a temporary basis during the pendency of the divorce litigation

2. Rehabilitative, transitional, or short term alimony—Support is issued for a defined period to a needy spouse so that the needy spouse can within the defined time frame become self supporting. Many states require that the needy spouse show a plan to the court outlining a time frame and steps to be taken to ensure rehabilitation before granting such an award

3. Reimbursement alimony—This type of alimony is usually awarded to compensate a spouse who supported their spouse through an endeavour such as enhanced education, for instance, law school in anticipation of sharing in the enhanced earning capacity.

4. Bridge-the-gap or limited duration alimony—This type of alimony is only recognized by a few states and is usually issued in short term marriages. In addition this type of alimony is for a very short time frame usually defined in months and directed for a sole purpose, such as car payments for a limited duration, or initial expenses to settle into a new household. This alimony is solely meant to bridge the gap between married and single status.

5. Permanent, indefinite, or periodic alimony—Unlike the other types of alimony discussed above this award of alimony terminates only upon the death of the paying spouse or the remarriage of the receiving spouse. Courts will only issue such an award of alimony when it is determined that the needy spouse lacks the ability to become financially self supporting.

6. Lump sum alimony—Lump sum alimony is not modifiable, and once an award is issued the person receiving such an award has a vested interest in the award and therefore such obligation will not terminate upon the death of the paying spouse or upon a contingent event such as the remarriage of the needy

spouse. Lump sum alimony is a fixed amount of alimony, though it can be order to be paid in installments over time.

7. Nominal alimony—Nominal alimony is an award of alimony for a *de minimus* amount, giving the court jurisdiction to modify the alimony amount in the future, due to some sort of forseeable circumstance, such as a degenerative illness by the spouse who will need alimony, or the freeing up of income, by a payor spouse who will be burdened with child support payments for a period of time.

POLICY—The general policy behind alimony is to allow an otherwise dependent spouse to become economically self sufficient. Therefore, permanent, indefinite or periodic alimony is rarely granted and is granted generally only when the court finds that the issuance of another type of alimony will never be sufficient to rehabilitate a needy spouse so that he or she can eventually become self-supporting.

3. **What Type of Alimony Should Be Issued?**

Main Factors:

a. **Length of Marriage:** When issuing a type and award of alimony courts in some jurisdictions will look to the length of the marriage. The courts will generally require a showing that the parties were engaged in a long term marriage.

b. **Economic Circumstances of the Parties**

    (a) earning capacity

    (b) education

    (c) health

    (d) nonmarital resources

    (e) age

        i. **Effect of Valid Separation or Antenuptial Agreement:** In general, if a court finds that a valid separation or antenuptial agreement governs alimony, then it will abide by the agreement unless it finds that the provisions violate public policy. This may result in higher or lower alimony than the court might otherwise order.

        ii. **Amount of Alimony:** The amount of alimony is within the court's discretion. Some states have enacted statutory tables to determine the amount the court will consider the financial resources of the parties, the standard of living of the couple, the time it takes for the party seeking alimony to get gainful employment, the duration of the marriage, the condition of the spouse seeking alimony (including age, physical and emotional health) and the ability of the party from whom alimony is sought to meet his or her own needs as well as the needs of the party seeking alimony.

(a) **Role of Fault:** The role of fault varies by state. In some states, it has no role at all and may not be considered by the court. In other states, particularly those which still preserve fault grounds, it may be considered.

iii. **Modification to Award:** Assuming an award of alimony, the court may modify that award if it reserves jurisdiction or the state statute permits modification. The predominant justification is that one of the partner's circumstances has changed substantially from the time the original award of alimony was issued. Thus, if the recipient partner has changed needs, or the paying partner has changed ability to pay, the court may, but is not required to, modify the award. The court may also modify the award in the event of fraud or mistake.

iv. **Termination of Award:** Typically, the obligation to pay alimony ends upon the death of either spouse. This general rule may also be modified by the terms of a valid separation or antenuptial agreement, which may trigger a lump sum payment or impose a separate obligation to fund a life insurance policy in favor of the recipient spouse. The alimony obligation also frequently, but not inevitably, ends upon the remarriage of the recipient partner. In the event that the recipient spouse cohabits with another individual, many states have enacted statutes that provide for a decrease (downward modification) or termination of the alimony award altogether. The obligation may not be discharged in bankruptcy, although the changed financial circumstances of the paying partner may justify a change in the award.

c. **Child Support**

i. **Past Trends:** In the past, the mother typically received custody of the children in a divorce, and the father had the duty to support them.

ii. **Current Status:** Today, of course, both parents are obligated to support their children. The amount of child support paid is usually calculated based on the number of children and the financial resources of each parent.

(a) **Methods of Calculation:** All states now have statutory guidelines under which they calculate the amount of child support that a parent must pay. These guidelines generally require a non-custodial parent to contribute a set percentage of his or her income to the children.

(b) **Assets and Alimony:** In determining the amount of child support a parent is obligated to pay, court may look at the alimony and assets each parent received in the property distribution.

(c) **Child's Reasonable Needs:** Parents are required to meet the reasonable needs of their children, and these reasonable needs are considered when the court orders child support. Although it may seem counterintuitive, a child's reasonable needs are usually based upon the child's lifestyle prior to the divorce. In other words, a court will usually order parents who are able to do so to support the child in the style to which the child has become accustomed. The public policy reason behind this standard is to ensure that children are not financially penalized by their parents' divorce. For example, if a child were attending private school during the marriage the court may order the parents to continue paying for private school in a child support order after the dissolution of marriage.

(d) **Time Frame**

- **Temporary Support:** Temporary support is support that the non-custodial parent pays while the divorce is still pending and before there has been a permanent child support order from the court.

- **Permanent Support:** After the divorce is final, parents are required to support their children until the children reach the age of 18 or until some other agreed-upon or statutorily mandated date (sometimes the child's graduation from college or marriage before a certain age). Of course, if a child has some disability or incapacity that prevents her from supporting herself, parents may be required to support that child indefinitely.

- **Retroactive Support:** Many states will order a lump sum of child support to be paid out over time, representing the period of time that the parents did not live together that was prior to either party filing an action seeking child support.

(e) **Changes in Orders:** Child support is modifiable. Parents may petition the court to change the amount of child support they are required to pay when their financial circumstances significantly change. Either parent may so petition the court. In other words, if a parent's income dramatically decreases, that parent may ask the court to lower the payments. However, if there is a substantial increase in income or the child's needs, a parent may ask the court to increase payments. As such petitions merely reflect the requirements of child support guidelines, they are typically granted if supported by the evidence.

VI. CHILD CUSTODY

A. **OVERVIEW:** There are two types of child custody. Many states are shying away from the use of the term "custody," which is a term traditionally used to describe property. However, the federal statutes previously discussed still use the term custody when dealing with child-related issues.

1. **Legal Custody:** When a parent shares legal custody of a child, a parent may not have physical custody, but retains the right and responsibility to make joint decisions regarding the child's education, health care, and religion. A parent may also impose rules and discipline on the child and participate in the child's care. Legal custody is also called parental responsibility.

2. **Physical Custody:** A parent who has physical custody actually lives with the child. Because many parents have arrangements where the child(ren) spend time with both parents, some states will designate the parents are the primary residential parent and the secondary residential parent. Parents who spend equal amounts of time with the children are called co-primary residential parents.

3. **Relationship Between Legal and Physical Custody:** A parent who has either legal or physical custody or both necessarily has the power. Major decisions on topics such as education, health care, and religion are expected to be decided by the parent with legal custody. If the parents have joint legal custody, then those major decisions are shared. Regardless of who has "legal custody," day-to-day decisions are decided by the parent who has physical custody of the child at that moment, such as what the child will eat and wear that day to act in the child's best interests as described under the concept of legal custody.

4. **Joint Custody:** Joint custody can refer to the decision-making authority or the residential arrangements for the child. Joint custody may require the parents to arrange for the child to live with each parent for some set period of time per year. It may also simply require that both parents have legal custody of the child, while one parent retains physical custody.

5. **Parenting Plans:** Many states have done away with the entire concept of custody and instead have established the concept of a parenting plan where parents share all decision making over the children and have a schedule of contact and access that does not favor either parent.

B. STANDARD FOR AWARDING CUSTODY

1. **Test:** All courts now employ the "best interests of the child" test when determining legal and physical custody. Many factors may enter into the analysis, including the role of each parent in raising and caring for the child up to the time of the divorce, the parents' behavior in society (if the parents' behavior would affect the child, as in the case of violent tendencies), and the parents' physical and emotional health. However, the court should not consider the race of the parents or the parents' financial circumstances (because finances can be addressed through support orders). Some courts permit the consideration of sexual orientation or religion, although most that do consider religion only to the extent that it affects the child's secular well-being. When a child is old

enough to contribute meaningfully to the court's analysis, the child's opinion and requests may enter into a custody determination.

2. **State Requirements**

   a. **Agreements:** Most states will recognize parents' agreements as to custody. Of course, where the parents reach an agreement about a child's custody, the court must review that agreement to make sure that the agreement was voluntary and takes into account the best interests of the child.

   b. **Joint Custody:** Some states require the parents to share custody absent some compelling reason to the contrary.

   c. **Custody to Natural Parents:** All states recognize the right of natural parents to have custody of their children. This right will only be overridden by some compelling reason, such as a lack of fitness on the part of the natural parents. Therefore, even if a person other than the natural parent might be better able to care for the children, this will not be enough to remove the child from the natural parent's care.

C. WHEN CUSTODY CHANGES

1. **Best Interests of the Child:** Custody of children (both the legal and physical aspects) are subject to modification. However, a court will only change its custody order if to do so is in the best interests of the child. Usually, given the fact that children need stability, this will only be the case if there have been some major changes in circumstances that necessitate a change in custody.

D. RIGHTS TO VISITATION

1. **Presumptions — Parents:** In all states, non-custodial parents are presumed to have the right to visit their natural children. Both parents and children are said to benefit from this arrangement. Of course, where visitation could be emotionally or physically harmful to the child, such visitation may be prohibited, or the court may order that it be supervised. Many states have also done away with the term visitation and refer to time spent with the child as time-sharing or contact and access.

2. **Grandparents**

   a. **Historically:** Historically, grandparents had no right to visit their grandchildren in the face of parental objection. Until recently, many courts would have applied the "best interests of the child" test in determining whether grandparents could visit their grandchildren. Other courts might have employed a stricter standard and examined whether separation from their grandparents would be harmful to the grandchildren.

    b. **Current Status:** The Supreme Court held, in 2000, that fit parents have a fundamental right to control who visits with their children, even if the proposed visitors are blood relatives (other than the parents themselves). Today, though all states have a third party visitation statute that permits grandparents to petition the court for visitation, under current Supreme Court law, grandparents have few, if any, visitation rights.

3. **Other People:** As stated above, parents have a constitutional right to decide who visits with their children. Therefore, unless the person petitioning for visitation has some close connection to the child (like a sibling or a long-term stepparent) such that to deprive the child of visitation would be demonstrably harmful, a parent will likely be able to prohibit such visitation.

E. RIGHTS OF VISITING PARENTS

1. **Discipline:** Visiting non-custodial parents may discipline their children as they see fit.

2. **Activities:** Visiting non-custodial parents may decide which activities their children will engage in.

    CAVEAT: Both of these rights are subject, of course, to the understanding that a visiting parent may not place his child in danger or do things that go strongly against the child's best interests.

VII. TERMINATION OF PARENTAL RIGHTS

A. **OVERVIEW:** Generally, it is quite difficult to terminate a natural parent's parental rights absent their consent.

1. **Voluntary Termination:** Of course, a parent may choose voluntarily to terminate her parental rights. This generally occurs when a parent wishes to place a child for adoption. Note that a court will usually look carefully to make sure that such consent is truly voluntary and will usually allow a parent to revoke consent within a short time after granting it.

2. **Involuntary Termination:** A natural parent's parental rights will only be involuntarily terminated if the parent is unfit in some way. Generally, in order to find a parent unfit, a court must find at least by clear and convincing evidence that the parent has neglected or abused their child.

VIII. ADOPTION

A. **OVERVIEW:** Adoption is the process by which someone other than the natural parent of the child becomes the child's legal parent.

B. PREREQUISITE—DEATH TERMINATION OF PARENTAL RIGHTS: A child is eligible for adoption upon the death of both of his natural parents. Of course, if one or both natural parents are living, the parental rights of the living natural parents must be terminated before a child is free for adoption. This termination may occur either voluntarily or involuntarily.

C. PARTIES

1. **Adoptive Parents:** In most states, adults may only adopt children, though in some states adults may adopt other adults. While many states permit unmarried persons to adopt, a few states openly prohibit homosexuals from adopting.

   a. **Family:** When both parents have died, or when a parent's parental rights have been terminated, the court will generally look to see whether there are biological relatives who are willing and able to adopt the child.

   b. **Others:** Where there are no biological family members who are willing and able to adopt the child, or, in the case of a voluntary termination or death of a parent, where the natural parent has specified that an unrelated individual should adopt the child, the court may allow an unrelated person to adopt. In the case of involuntary terminations of parental rights, foster parents who have cared for the child may be particularly appropriate adoptive parents.

2. **Adoptees:** Children are eligible for adoption if their parents are deceased or have had their parental rights terminated. In some states, and under the Uniform Adoption Act, adults may also be adopted. In some jurisdictions, older children may give consent to be adopted, but the adoption may occur absent their consent if the court determines that adoption would be in the best interests of the child.

D. RESTRICTIONS ON ADOPTION: Some states, will consider whether the child has the same religion or race as the proposed adoptive parents in evaluating a proposed petition to adopt only parents of the same religion as the child may adopt.

E. RELATIONSHIP OF ADOPTED CHILDREN TO ADOPTIVE FAMILIES: Once an adoption is complete, an adopted child is considered to have equal status to a natural child.

F. RELATIONSHIP OF ADOPTED CHILDREN TO BIOLOGICAL FAMILIES: Once an adoption is complete, an adopted child maintains no legal connection to his biological family.

IX. REPRODUCTIVE TECHNOLOGIES

A. OVERVIEW: As scientific technology develops and improves, new issues arise in the law about the legal rights and duties of persons who choose to conceive children in other than the traditional way. Because technology now makes it possible for a woman to carry a child that is biologically related neither to her nor to her husband, a child born thanks to reproductive technology techniques may have several people who claim to be her parents. This section will address a few of the situations in which legal issues as to parentage may arise.

1. **In Vitro Fertilization, Surrogacy, and Parenthood**

   a. **In General:** Because it is now possible for doctors to harvest eggs from a woman, fertilize them outside the body (in vitro), and then implant them into a woman's uterus, all kinds of legal issues may arise.

   b. **Legitimacy:** Most states now consider a child conceived through in vitro fertilization to be legitimate.

   c. **Legal Parenthood:** Who may claim to be the legal parent of a child conceived through in vitro fertilization is certainly an issue that currently concerns many lawyers and scholars. For example, if a woman's own egg is fertilized outside of her body and then implanted back into her uterus, then she is obviously the legal mother of the child. However, there are at least three other possibilities:

      A donor egg (the egg of another woman) is implanted into a woman's uterus, and she then gives birth to the child and claims it as her own, or

      The woman's own egg is implanted into a surrogate's uterus with the intention that the surrogate will relinquish the baby upon birth to the woman, or

      A donor egg is implanted into a surrogate's uterus with the intention that the surrogate will relinquish the baby upon birth to the woman.

   The same issues arise when it is not the egg, but the sperm that is at issue. Here, there are also many possibilities:

      Donor sperm (the sperm of another man) is used to inseminate a woman's egg (either through artificial insemination or through in vitro fertilization), and she then gives birth to the child and the couple claims the child as their own, or

      The man's own sperm is used to inseminate a surrogate's egg (either through artificial insemination or through in vitro fertilization), and the surrogate carries the baby to term with the intention that the surrogate will relinquish the baby upon birth to the man and his wife, or

      Donor sperm is used to inseminate a surrogate's egg (either through artificial insemination or through in vitro fertilization), and the surrogate carries the baby to term with the intention that the surrogate will relinquish the baby upon birth to the man and his wife, or

Donor sperm and a donor egg fertilized via in vitro fertilization, implanted into a surrogate's uterus, and the surrogate carries the baby to term with the intention that the surrogate will relinquish the baby upon birth to the man and his wife, or

Donor sperm and a donor egg are implanted into the wife's uterus (either through artificial insemination or through in vitro fertilization), and the wife carries the baby to term with the intention that she and her husband will claim the baby as their own and raise it.

i. **Contractual View:** When surrogates, donor eggs, or donor sperm are used, the issue becomes who is the legal parent of the resulting child. Most agencies and attorneys now require surrogates and sperm or egg donors to waive all parental rights to any resulting child prior to surrogacy or donation. However, states vary in their approaches to enforcing such contracts. Certainly, a contract with a surrogate, for example, is more likely to be enforced when the surrogate has no biological relationship to the child (i.e., when a donor egg and donor sperm, or the wife's egg and husband's sperm, are used).

ii. **Custody View:** On occasion, when faced with a conflict between biological parents (i.e, the ones who provided the sperm or egg or carried the child) and contracting parents (i.e., the ones who arranged for the child's conception and intended to be its "parents"), courts have treated contractual arrangements simply as custody-type situations. In these cases, the courts have used the typical "best interests of the child" test in determining who should have custody of the resulting child.

iii. **Baby Selling:** One issue that frequently arises in the area of surrogacy and egg or sperm donation is the concept of baby selling. All states prohibit the selling of human beings, and there is a strong public policy rationale against the selling of babies for adoption or otherwise. Therefore, contracts for surrogacy or donation must be carefully worded to avoid even the appearance of impropriety or illegality.

iv. **Discarding or Implantation of Frozen Embryos:** Because in vitro fertilization technology allows embryos to be frozen, several legal issues may arise.

(a) **Donation of Embryos:** Most states allow couples to donate any unused embryos to another couple. In situation, the law will treat the recipient couple in the same way that surrogates are treated in the above analysis.

(b) **Discarding of Embryos:** At least one case has arisen in which a couple divorced and still had embryos frozen. In this case, the husband wished to donate the embryos to other infertile couples. The wife wished to discard the embryos, saying that she did not want to become a parent to any future children with the husband. The court ruled in favor of the wife, saying that, in this case, the wife's right not to procreate outweighed the husband's wish to procreate through the frozen embryos, especially in light of the fact that the husband was able to procreate naturally and could father future children even without the embryos.

1. Common Law Marriage

2. Constitutional Right to Marry

3. Constitutional Right of Same-Sex Couples to Marry

4. Constitutional Right of Same-Sex Couples to Marry

5. Right to Procreation

6. Marriage Licenses

7. Requirements to Obtain a Marriage License

8. Requirements to Obtain a Marriage License

9. Marriage Ceremony Requirements

10. Marriage License Requirements

11. Requirements for Officiants

12. Covenant Marriage

13. Common Law Marriage

14. Impediments to Marriage

15. Conflict of Laws

16. Divorce – Formal Marriage

17. Voiding of a Marriage

18. Marriage Between Family Members

19. Consanguinity Statutes

20. Minimum Age Requirements for Marriage

21. Pregnancy as a Waiver of Age Requirement

22. Remarriage Upon Divorce

23. Right of Mentally Ill People to Marry

24. Impotence as a Grounds for Divorce

25. Right for Prisoners to Marry

26. Return of Engagement Ring

55. Marital Assets – Distribution

56. Marital Assets – Distribution

57. Alimony

58. Alimony

59. Alimony

60. Alimony

61. Child Support

62. Child Support

63. Child Support

64. Post-Nuptial Agreements

65. Child Support

66. Child Support

67. Child Custody

68. Tender Years Statutes

69. Child Custody

70. Child Custody

71. Child Custody

72. Child Custody

73. Child Custody

74. Child Custody

75. Joint Custody

76. Child Custody

77. Grandparent Visitation

78. Visitation – Right for Non-Custodial Parent to Make Decisions

79. Duty to Pay Child Support

TRUE-FALSE QUESTIONS

(Circle Correct Answer)

1. **T F** Most states recognize common law marriage.

2. **T F** Under the Constitution, there is a fundamental right to marry.

3. **T F** The Fourteenth Amendment guarantees same sex couples the right to marry.

4. **T F** In Hawaii and Vermont, same sex couples can marry.

5. **T F** Even if a person cannot support a child who is not in his custody, he is still free to remarry and have more children.

6. **T F** Marriage licenses are required in most states.

7. **T F** Blood tests for sexually transmitted diseases as a requirement to obtain a marriage license are permissible because they work to protect children and are minimally intrusive.

8. **T F** Waiting periods for licenses are valid.

9. **T F** A member of a couple need not attend his or her own marriage ceremony.

10. **T F** Even if a couple does not get a marriage license, a marriage will still be valid.

11. **T F** A marriage is valid even if the officiant is not legally allowed to perform marriage ceremonies.

12. **T F** In a case of covenant marriage, a state can impose stricter divorce laws.

13. **T F** All that is required for a common law marriage is that the "spouses" live together for a statutorily designated period of time.

14. **T F** If a marriage had an impediment at the outset, it must be invalidated.

15. **T F** Under conflict of law principles, a couple that is not married but meets all of the requirements for a common law marriage in one state may be married in another state, even if the other state doesn't permit common law marriage.

16. **T F** Even where there is no formal marriage, a couple must still get divorced.

17. **T F** Where there is an impediment to a marriage, a judicial declaration is required to void the marriage.

18. **T F** Most states allow marriage between first cousins.

19. **T F** Under a consanguinity statute, adopted family members are treated just as blood relatives are.

20. **T F** Most states statutorily dictate only one minimum age for obtainment of a marriage license.

21. **T F** In determining whether an underage couple may marry, the fact that the female is pregnant is dispositive.

22. **T F** Because a divorce ends the marriage, parties may remarry immediately upon the granting of a divorce.

23. **T F** Mentally ill people cannot marry.

24. **T F** Concealment of impotence is grounds for divorce.

25. **T F** Prisoners may be forbidden to marry.

26. **T F** If the man breaks off the engagement, the woman is entitled to keep her engagement ring.

27. **T F** A testator may require a beneficiary to marry in order to receive a gift under the will.

28. **T F** Civil unions are available in all states for same sex couples.

29. **T F** An annulment applies to a problem that existed at the time the parties entered into the marriage contract.

30. **T F** When a marriage has been annulled, the children are considered to be illegitimate.

31. **T F** The federal courts have jurisdiction over divorces.

32. **T F** Under the right to travel, a person may travel to any state to obtain a divorce.

33. **T F** In order to obtain a divorce on the basis of cruelty, a spouse need not demonstrate that there has been physical abuse by the other spouse.

34. **T F** In order to be separated, the parties need not actually live apart.

35. **T F** Where desertion is a grounds for divorce, an uninterrupted statutory period must occur.

36. **T F** Only a husband may be charged with non-support.

37. **T F** If a spouse was intoxicated at the time he/she committed adultery, then the plaintiff's spouse will have no grounds for adultery.

38. **T F** If a spouse is "habitually" intoxicated, the other spouse may bring an action for divorce.

39. **T F** Impotence is grounds for divorce.

40. **T F** When a spouse is convicted of a felony, the other spouse may sue for divorce.

41. **T F** Most states have grounds for divorce on basis of irreconcilable differences.

42. **T F** All states have no-fault divorce.

43. **T F** There will be no grounds for divorce if one spouse consents to the other spouse's conduct that ordinarily would be grounds for divorce.

44. **T F** If parties want to come to a financial arrangement, they can only do so through divorce, not separation.

45. **T F** Mere incompatibility is sufficient grounds for a legal separation.

46. T F Restraining orders to prevent domestic abuse are usually enforceable from state to state.

47. T F Alimony is only available in the case of a divorce, not an annulment.

48. T F Before a divorce is final, a court may issue orders designed to protect the children of the marriage.

49. T F Each spouse must always pay his own fees for a divorce.

50. T F Most states follow an equitable distribution scheme in dividing the marital assets.

51. T F Marital property generally includes property that is inherited by the spouses during the marriage.

52. T F Some states do not recognize assets acquired before the marriage as individual property.

53. T F All states recognize that, where a spouse has supported the other in obtaining a professional degree, the supporting spouse should receive an interest in that degree or license in divorce.

54. T F Debts or liabilities incurred by the spouses are also subject to equitable distribution in divorce.

55. T F The spouse who is at fault in the divorce is likely to receive fewer marital assets.

56. T F If the parties choose to divide their property themselves, the courts will generally honor those agreements.

57. T F Only wives are entitled to alimony.

58. T F The spouse that is at fault in a divorce is likely to receive less alimony.

59. T F When a spouse remarries, he is generally no longer entitled to receive alimony.

60. T F Alimony is a debt dischargeable in a bankruptcy.

61. T F In the case of a divorce, both parents are obligated to pay child support.

62. T F Courts look at the standard of living that a child would have had had divorce not occurred in determining child support.

63. T F If a child does not obey his parents, he may not receive child support.

64. T F Post-nuptial agreements are considered to be enforceable.

65. T F Under federal law, an employer can withhold child support from an employee's paycheck.

66. T F It is crime not to support one's children.

67. T F There are two types of custody in a divorce situation.

68. **T** **F** "Tender Years" statutes still exist in most states.

69. **T** **F** A child may participate in the decision of which parent he should reside with.

70. **T** **F** If a parent who seeks custody is guilty of misconduct, this will be a factor in the custody determination.

71. **T** **F** If the custody-seeking parent is residing with a person to whom s/he is not married, the court will take this fact into account in making a custody determination.

72. **T** **F** A parent who is open to visitation and does everything possible to encourage and allow visitation by the non-custodial parent is more likely to receive custody.

73. **T** **F** When making custody decisions, the court should take the parents' religion into account.

74. **T** **F** The court may properly consider race of parents and children when making custody decisions.

75. **T** **F** Joint custody is generally presumed in divorce situations.

76. **T** **F** The best interests of the child always controls who has custody of the child.

77. **T** **F** Grandparents have a fundamental right to visit their grandchildren.

78. **T** **F** During visitation, a non-custodial parent may make decisions for his or her child.

79. **T** **F** If a natural parent is not allowed to visit his child, he does not have to pay child support.

ANSWERS TO TRUE-FALSE QUESTIONS

1. False

Only a few states currently recognize common law marriage.

2. True

The Fourteenth Amendment guarantees a fundamental right to marriage. Any significant restriction on this right is subject to a strict scrutiny analysis. However, a minor restriction, such as an age requirement or a requirement for a blood test, is only subject to rational basis scrutiny.

3. False

While the Fourteenth Amendment does guarantee a fundamental right to marry, this right has not been applied to marriages between two men or two women. Note that the Supreme Judicial court of the State of Massachusetts has recognized a right to same sex marriage under the Massachusetts State Constitution, and several states permit same sex couples to enter into civil unions or domestic partnerships.

4. False

In Hawaii, the legislature has outlawed same sex marriage (see answer to previous question). In Vermont, same sex couples are granted a right to civil union, but not to marriage.

5. True

An inability to meet one's financial obligations is not a valid basis for a significant restriction on a fundamental right to marry.

6. True

Licenses are generally used to determine whether persons are eligible to marry. For example, same sex couples or persons who are already married to others will not be granted licenses to marry.

7. True

Blood tests are required in many states; however, most states will still grant a license even if one partner has a sexually transmitted disease, as long as the other partner knows about it.

8. True

A state can impose a waiting period for a couple to obtain a marriage license, as long as that waiting period is not too long.

9. True

Such a marriage is called a marriage by proxy. Under ordinary circumstances, both members of the couple must be physically present for the marriage ceremony. However, under the marriage by proxy theory, which is usually applied when one member of the couple is stationed in the military overseas or is incarcerated, a marriage ceremony may be valid where an agent stands in for the absent spouse.

10. True

Most state courts have held that, where a couple has a marriage ceremony, such a ceremony usually results in a valid marriage, even where they have not obtained a valid marriage license. This is especially true where one member of the couple believed that the license was valid.

11. True

However, at least one member of the couple must have had a good faith belief that the officiant was legally authorized. This type of marriage is usually called a putative marriage.

12. True

When parties enter into a covenant marriage, they make deeper commitments than those in a typical marriage. Therefore, some states have enacted stricter grounds for obtaining a divorce in covenant marriages.

13. False

In most states, it is not the period of time for which a couple lives together that is dispositive; rather, the court will look to whether a couple has an intent to be married and holds itself out to the public as a married couple.

14. False

If an impediment (such as a prior existing marriage) is eventually removed, then the marriage may be affirmed. Note that this is also true in the case of common law marriages.

15. True

If a couple was considered to be married under the common law in another state, most states will recognize the marriage, even if the state in which the couple is currently residing does not recognize common law marriages.

16. **True**

Even where a couple has not been married with a ceremony and a license, if a common law marriage is deemed to exist, then the couple is deemed to have all the rights of an officially married couple. Therefore, in order to terminate the marriage, the couple must formally divorce.

17. **False**

Because a void marriage is a nullity under legal and public policy principles, a court need not invalidate it. The spouses themselves may simply declare the marriage to be terminated.

18. **True**

Even though virtually all states prohibit marriages between parents and children, grandparents and grandchildren, brothers and sisters, uncles/aunts and nephews/nieces, in many states first cousins are allowed to marry.

19. **True**

The purpose behind consanguinity statutes is not only to prevent congenital abnormalities in the children of the marriage; rather, such statutes are also intended to carry on social and religious traditions. Therefore, even where there is no blood relationship, adopted children are treated the same as naturally born children.

20. **False**

Most states have two statutorily established ages: one before which people can marry only with parental or judicial permission and one above which they are deemed to be capable of consenting to a marriage.

21. **False**

While some courts take this factor into account, it will not be the sole basis for a court's decision to allow underage persons to marry.

22. **False**

Some jurisdictions impose a waiting period of up to several months, during which time the spouses are not yet free to remarry.

23. **False**

If a person is mentally competent at the time of the actual marriage ceremony (i.e., the mentally ill person understood the nature of the marriage contract and gave voluntary consent), the marriage will be deemed to be valid.

24. True

It may also be grounds for an annulment. Note that it is not a requirement for marriage that the marriage be consummated; rather, it is the concealment of inability to consummate the marriage that constitutes grounds for the annulment or divorce.

25. False

Although the United State Supreme Court does not apply a strict scrutiny standard of review to prison inmate marriages, a prison may pass a regulation prohibiting inmates to marry only if that regulation is reasonably related to legitimate prison objectives.

26. False

Most jurisdictions now hold that the man may recover the engagement ring even if the breakup of the engagement was his own fault.

27. True

The only type of marriage requirement that is absolutely prohibited is a total restraint on marriage. An inducement to marry, even where the testator places restrictions or requirements on that marriage, may be viewed as valid.

28. False

However, in several states same-sex couples may enter into civil unions or domestic partnerships affording them the same rights and benefits as marriage.

29. True

In order to obtain an annulment, the parties must generally prove that, at the time of the marriage, because of some defect, the marriage was void or voidable.

30. False

In general, because most states are leaning toward rendering children legitimate, a child born of a void or voidable marriage will be considered to be legitimate under the Uniform Marriage and Divorce Act.

31. False

Federal courts do not have jurisdiction to hear divorce cases. In fact, most states have family or divorce courts which deal specifically in the area of family law.

32. False

Many states have residential requirements of six months to one year before a person can obtain a divorce in a state. The Supreme Court has upheld these residential requirements as constitutional.

33. True

Threats will generally be enough if they place the petitioner spouse in fear that physical violence will occur and affect the health of the petitioner spouse in some way.

34. True

While physical absence will, of course, constitute a separation, so will living apart within the same residence or even refusal to participate in the marriage, such as refusal to engage in sexual relations.

35. True

If the deserting spouse returns or makes a good faith offer to return, the period is deemed to be interrupted, and the plaintiff's spouse will not be able to bring an action for desertion.

36. False

Although in the past, only a wife could charge a husband with failure to support her, modernly, the courts will allow either spouse to bring such a claim.

37. False

Voluntarily intoxication is not an excuse for adultery.

38. True

Most states recognize that, where a spouse regularly and excessively uses drugs or alcohol, it is grounds for divorce.

39. True

It may also be grounds for annulment if it was present at the time of the marriage contract. Note, however, that impotence means an inability to engage in sexual intercourse. It does not mean an inability to procreate.

40. True

In most states the conviction of a serious crime or a prison sentence will be grounds for divorce.

41. True

Note that, in most states, both spouses must agree that the marriage has irretrievably broken down. However, in some states, only one spouse must so allege.

42. True

Since the mid-1980s, all states have allowed no-fault divorces, either through the grounds of irreconcilable differences or by allowing the couple to separate and then file for divorce. However, note that many states have began to wonder whether no-fault divorce makes divorce too easy to procure, and some commentators are wondering whether the trends toward allowing no-fault divorces may reverse.

43. True

This is called connivance. Connivance is particularly applicable in the case of adultery. Therefore, if one spouse allows the other spouse to commit adultery, adultery will not be grounds for divorce.

44. False

Even spouses who are only separated, not divorced, may enter into a separation agreement that makes provisions for their financial settlement.

45. False

Because the interest of the state is in preserving marriage, the couple must prove irreconcilable differences, not merely incompatibility.

46. True

Under the Full Faith and Credit Clause, most states will recognize the restraining orders issued by other states.

47. False

Most states award alimony in annulment situations as well as in divorces.

48. True

While these orders are temporary pending the finalization of the divorce, courts have a vested interest in ensuring that children are well cared for, both financially and emotionally, while a divorce is pending.

49. False

Indeed, courts often order a spouse with more extensive resources to pay the fees of the other spouse so that the divorce may proceed.

50. True

While there are a few community property states, the remainder of the states generally follow an equitable distribution policy.

51. False

Marital property only includes property acquired by an individual or by both spouses during the marriage; it generally does not include inherited property.

52. True

In a few equitable distribution states, the court considers both property acquired during the marriage and property acquired before the marriage to be subject to equitable distribution principles. Note that, in these states, inherited property may become part of the marital assets in a divorce.

53. False

States are divided in whether a spouse may claim an interest in a professional degree or license belonging to the other spouse. Most states view the degree or license as belonging only to a holder to that license or degree and, therefore, it is not divisible under equitable distribution.

54. True

Most states divide both the assets and the liabilities of the marriage.

55. False

In an equitable distribution state, fault does not enter into the equitable distribution calculations unless the fault was extreme or caused the other spouse some financial detriment.

56. True

Examples of such contracts include prenuptial and antenuptial agreements.

57. False

The United States Supreme Court has held that gender-based alimony awards violate the Equal Protection Clause of the Fourteenth Amendment and are therefore unconstitutional.

58. False

The fault generally does not enter into alimony awards. Rather, the court awards alimony on a financial need basis.

59. True

Most states end alimony payments after the remarriage of the recipient spouse. In a case of remarriage, the court expects that the recipient and his or her new spouse will support each other.

60. False

Alimony is not considered to be a debt and, therefore, it is not dischargeable under bankruptcy laws.

61. True

Child support is no longer the responsibility of solely the father; rather, both spouses must join in supporting their children to the best of their ability.

62. True

The standard of living the child would have enjoyed had the divorce not occurred is factored into a court's "reasonable needs" analysis.

63. True

Many courts have held that the receipt of child support is contingent upon the child obeying and complying with the reasonable regulations of his or her parents.

64. True.

Just like antenuptial agreements, post-nuptial agreements are generally enforceable in the absence of duress or some other standard contract defense.

65. True

The Family Support Act of 1988 actually requires an employer to withhold child support from employee's payments. The purpose of the statute is to improve child support enforcement.

66. True

Under federal law, a parent must support children of the divorce to live in another state. If the parent has failed to pay child support for more than one year or owes more than $5,000, criminal sanctions apply.

67. True

Physical custody involves a child's physical residence with one or the other parent. Legal custody involves a parent's involvement with the child, including making of medical, legal, religious, disciplinary, educational, and other decisions.

68. False

Under "Tender Years" statutes, it was presumed that young children should live with their mother. Most states have abolished these statutes.

69. True

As long as the child is old enough to understand and make an intelligent choice, under the Uniform Marriage and Divorce Act, a judge may allow a child to offer an opinion and participate in the decision-making process.

70. False

The misconduct of a parent who is seeking custody is only relevant if that misconduct has application to the relationship between the parent and the child or otherwise affects the child.

71. False

The court will only take such a living arrangement into account if the arrangement is likely to adversely affect the child. This standard has been applied in both same sex and opposite sex living arrangements.

72. True

If one parent is unlikely to allow visitation by the non-custodial parent, custody will usually be granted to a parent who is willing to allow visitation to the non-custodial parent.

73. False

The most important determination is the child's welfare, although a court may take religion into account if it has a significant impact on the child.

74. False

The United States Supreme Court has ruled that a court may not consider racial differences in custody decisions.

75. False

There is a presumption in favor of joint custody in some states, but not in most. However, most states will look at the best interest of the child in deciding whether joint custody makes sense. Note that this is true even if neither parent petitions for joint custody.

76. False

Even though this statement sounds as if it should be true, note that natural parents are always given preference over other family members or unrelated persons. Note, of course, that where natural parents are unfit or where they request that custody go to an unrelated person, the court will generally remove the child from the natural parents.

77. False

The Supreme Court recently decided that parents are empowered with decision-making abilities regarding their children. Even if the parent decides to exclude a grandparent from a grandchild's upbringing, the parent's decision must be afforded some deference. Every state does have a third party visitation statute that permits grandparents to request that the court grant them visitation.

78. True

The custodial parent generally may not interfere unless the non-custodial parent is placing the child in some danger.

79. False

The duty to pay child support does not rely on the parent's ability to visit the child. Therefore, even where visitation is improperly disallowed, the parent still has a duty to pay child support and/or alimony.

MULTIPLE CHOICE QUESTIONS
TOPIC LIST

1. Marriage License Requirements

2. Full Faith and Credit – Marriage

3. Annulment

4. Void vs. Voidable Marriages

5. Common Law Marriage

6. Annulment/Divorce

7. Grounds for Divorce

8. Annulment

9. Residency – Divorce

10. Child Custody

11. Permanent Alimony

12. Rehabilitative Alimony

13. Distribution – Share of Professional Degree or License

14. Termination of Child Support

15. Annulment

16. Recognition of Divorce

17. Divorce – Cruelty

18. Divorce – Collusion

19. Custody by Natural Parents

20. Child Custody – Incapacity

21. Visitation by Non-Family Member

22. Visitation by Non-Biological Parent

23. Child Support

24. Rights and Responsibilities in Divorce

25. Responsibility of Primary Caretaker to Work Outside Home

Questions 1–3 refer to the following fact pattern.

Theresa and Henry are residents of State X. Theresa is 15 years old, and Henry is 29. For several months, since Theresa was 14, Theresa and Henry have been carrying on a torrid affair, during which Henry has told Theresa that, age aside, she is the love of his life. Theresa, who has admired Henry, her next-door neighbor, for years, is swept away by the affair and begins to do poorly in ninth grade because, rather than studying, she is hanging out with Henry.

In State X, it is legal for 15-year-old women to marry. As soon as she turns 15, Henry convinces Theresa to sneak out of her house one night and go to a justice of the peace. The justice of the peace marries them.

1. Assume for the purposes of this question only that Henry forged a marriage license before going to the justice of the peace. Because Theresa is 15, they could have obtained a real marriage license, but Henry was afraid that the clerk at the courthouse would call Theresa's parents and notify them of Henry's intention to marry their daughter.

    Is Theresa's marriage to Henry likely to be valid?

    (A) Yes, if both consent to the marriage and all other legal requirements are met.
    (B) Yes, if the parties wanted to be married.
    (C) No, because a valid marriage license is a legal requirement.
    (D) No, because the justice of the peace did not know of the falsity of the license.

2. Assume for the purposes of this question only that Theresa and Henry obtained a legitimate marriage license in State X. After being married for two years, Theresa and Henry decide to move to State Y because they have wanted to live near the ocean and State Y is a coastal state. Upon moving to State Y, they learn that a State Y statute requires people to be 18 to be legally married.

    What is the status of their marriage after they move?

    (A) The marriage is valid in State X, but not State Y.
    (B) The marriage is no longer valid in State X and is not valid.
    (C) The marriage is valid in both State X and State Y.
    (D) To answer, one needs more information about parental consent.

3. Assume for the purposes of this question only that Theresa's parents, after learning that Henry had been engaged in a sexual affair with Theresa for two months, threatened Henry with prosecution for statutory rape if he did not marry Theresa. Henry, who was terrified of going to jail, agreed. After two weeks of marriage, Henry now seeks to annul the marriage. As his attorney, you should advise him that

    (A) Henry entered the marriage under duress and is thus entitled to an annulment.
    (B) The marriage is voidable by Henry because of duress but only through a legal divorce.
    (C) The marriage is valid because duress can only be based on threats of physical violence.
    (D) The marriage is valid because they actually intended to have him thrown in jail.

FAMILY LAW

Questions 4–5 refer to the following fact pattern.

Alison and Bob are two adults living in the state of Argentia. They have been married for ten years. At the time of their marriage, Alison and Bob obtained a marriage license and were married with all requisite formalities in a marriage ceremony.

4. Assume for the purposes of this question only that Bob has recently died. Which of the following would be true?

   (A) If Alison and Bob were brother and sister, the marriage would have been voidable at any time.
   (B) If Alison and Bob were brother and sister, the marriage would have been voidable before Bob's death, but not after.
   (C) If Alison were previously married and never divorced, her marriage to Bob was void *ab initio*.
   (D) If Alison were previously married and never divorced, the marriage is voidable only before Bob dies.

5. Assume for the purposes of this question only that Alison and Bob were not brother and sister and are currently both alive. Furthermore, they have been living together for ten years, calling themselves husband and wife, and owning a home together. However, they have never obtained a marriage license, nor have they ever had an official marriage ceremony.

   Are Alison and Bob legally married?

   (A) Yes, provided that the state in which they reside recognizes common law marriage.
   (B) Yes, but only in the state in which they reside.
   (C) No, because common law marriage still requires a license.
   (D) No, because common law marriage still requires a marriage ceremony.

Questions 6–8 refer to the following fact pattern.

Gary and Henrietta, residents of the state of Albertville, are involved in a serious relationship. They have been dating for approximately three months, during which time they have seen each other every day. However, Gary and Henrietta have done nothing more than hold hands. Gary has told Henrietta that, due to his strong religious beliefs, he does not believe in premarital sex and cannot engage in sexual relations until they are married. Gary has failed to disclose that he is both impotent and suffering from AIDS.

Deeply in love with Gary, and frustrated by his unwillingness to engage in sexual relations, Henrietta suggests to Gary that they marry. Gary, who is genuinely and deeply in love with Henrietta, agrees. They obtain a marriage license and hold a small ceremony which is officiated by a rabbi and attended by about 20 of their friends.

Gary and Henrietta then go on their honeymoon. While in Hawaii, Gary continually rejects Henrietta's sexual advances. Finally, after three days during which Henrietta is growing more and more frustrated and unhappy, Gary reveals to her that he cannot have sex with her because he is impotent and that he expects to die shortly due to his low T-cell count.

6. Assume for the purposes of this question only that Henrietta immediately seeks to terminate the marriage. As her attorney, you should advise her that

   (A) The marriage may be dissolved by either annulment or divorce.
   (B) The marriage may be dissolved only by annulment.
   (C) The marriage may be dissolved only by divorce.
   (D) The marriage was void *ab initio*.

7. Assume for the purposes of this question only that Henrietta, still madly in love with Gary, tells him that she does not care about his impotence or physical health. While in Hawaii on her honeymoon, she still feels that she wants to be married to him. However, when she returns home to Albertville three weeks later, she confides in her best friend about the state of her marriage. Her best friend convinces her to annul the marriage.

Henrietta comes to you for legal advice. You should advise her that

(A) She is restrained from seeking an annulment because she assented to the marriage after she became aware of the fraud.

(B) She is restrained from seeking an annulment because she has not demonstrated that the maladies are untreatable.

(C) She may not be able to rely on the AIDS disease in obtaining an annulment or divorce, but the impotence may still be valid grounds for annulment.

(D) She may neither divorce Gary nor obtain an annulment until she has been married to him for at least a year.

8. Assume for the purposes of this question only that Gary does not suffer from AIDS and that, after two months of marriage, Gary tells Henrietta that he is not actually impotent but that he is not interested in her in a sexual way. He says that he loves her deeply but finds her physically unattractive. Henrietta seeks to annul the marriage.

As her attorney you should advise her that

(A) She cannot obtain an annulment.

(B) She can obtain an annulment on the basis of fraud because Gary impliedly promised to engage in sexual relations with her.

(C) In order to obtain an annulment, Henrietta would have to show that Gary was actually impotent.

(D) She can obtain an annulment only if Gary expressly promised before marriage that he would engage in sexual relations with her after marriage.

9. Carter married Dolly in the state of Whiteacre. Carter then moved to the state of Blackacre after five years of marriage and has lived there for two years. He then initiated divorce proceedings in Blackacre. In Blackacre

(A) The divorce proceedings are not valid.

(B) The divorce proceedings are valid only if Dolly consents.

(C) The divorce proceedings are valid only if Dolly's attorney waives objection to jurisdiction.

(D) The proceedings are valid in any event.

10. Nancy and Fred, who are in the process of divorcing, have two children, Frances and Arthur. A dispute arises between them as to custody of the children. How will the court determine who should have custody?

(A) The court will decide custody based on relative income of the parents.
(B) The court will determine who was at fault in causing the divorce in deciding custody.
(C) The court will decide based on the best interests of the children.
(D) The court will exercise its own discretion and take into account any factor it thinks is important.

Questions 11–13 refer to the following fact pattern.

Sally is divorcing Larry after 15 years of marriage. Prior to their marriage, Sally had finished two years of college and wants to go back to finish her degree. Sally supported Larry through dental school. Larry is now a hugely successful dentist to the stars.

11. The best argument for the award of alimony to Sally is

(A) Larry's earning capacity compared to that of Sally is much larger.
(B) Sally has an equitable investment in Larry's education.
(C) Larry's philandering was the reason for the divorce.
(D) Sally is a woman and is presumed to be entitled to alimony.

12. The best argument for an award of rehabilitative alimony in jurisdictions that recognize it is

(A) Sally has an investment in Larry's education.
(B) Larry's philandering was the cause of the divorce.
(C) Sally needs temporary support until she is self-supporting.
(D) Sally is entitled to as much education as Larry.

13. Assume for the purposes of this question only that Sally argues in the divorce that she entitled to a "share" of Larry's dental license and practice through equitable distribution. Is she likely to succeed in this argument?

(A) Yes, because professional licenses are generally subject to equitable distribution under a theory that the supporting spouse did so through good will.
(B) Yes, because professional licenses are "marital property" and are generally distributed equitably along with other marital assets.
(C) No, because a professional license generally is not subject to equitable distribution because it is personal to the person who actually earned it.
(D) No, because professional licenses are never subject to equitable distribution.

14. The court awards child support. Which of the following is least likely to be a justification for termination of that support?

(A) The child comes of age.
(B) The other spouse becomes financially well-off.
(C) The payor-spouse dies.
(D) The child becomes self-sufficient.

15. Which of the following would not be grounds for annulment?

    (A) The husband stated before marriage that he wanted seven children and then revealed after the marriage that he had had a vasectomy and was therefore sterile.

    (B) The husband stated before marriage that he was an open-minded, liberal person and then revealed after the marriage that he actually currently was a white supremacist and had been one for ten years.

    (C) The husband stated before marriage that he was not addicted to drugs when in fact he was a heroin addict.

    (D) The wife told the husband before marriage that she had never been in jail when in fact she had served time for killing her previous husband.

16. In which of the following situations would a state not recognize a divorce?

    (A) Where both spouses went to the country of Alberta and requested the divorce under the divorce laws in effect there.

    (B) Where one spouse traveled to a foreign country to obtain a divorce and the other spouse was unaware of the divorce proceeding.

    (C) The divorce decree was issued in conformance with the laws of the state to which the two spouses traveled, but not in the state from which they left.

    (D) The divorce decree failed to recite that the spouses met the residency requirement of the state issuing the decree even though they had met such requirement.

Questions 17–18 refer to the following fact pattern.

Monty and Sarah have been married for twelve years. Until a year ago, they were happily married. Within the last year, Monty has been going through a midlife crisis. He has begun driving a red sports car, he has gotten hair implants, and he has begun hanging out at adult clubs with his close friend Hugh.

17. Sarah has become very unhappy and has decided to seek a divorce. If Sarah wishes to base her divorce on the grounds of cruelty in a state that permits such a ground, you as her attorney should advise her that which of the following would support her claim?

    I. Monty has insulted her frequently, using expletives and calling her a prostitute.
    II. Monty has refused to engage in sexual relations with her, telling her that he finds the women at the adult clubs much more attractive.
    III. Monty has criticized Sarah on a daily basis, telling her that she needs to lose weight, wear tighter clothing, and put on makeup. He has also told her that she must put up with his criticism because, if he leaves her, she will never find another man.
    IV. Monty has hit Sarah on four different occasions, breaking her nose on one occasion and bruising her on two others.

    (A) IV only.
    (B) I and III only.
    (C) II and IV only.
    (D) I, II, III, or IV.

18. Assume for the purposes of this question only that Monty and Sarah secretly agree that they want a divorce. Assume also that Sarah is not a prostitute. However, Monty and Sarah live in a state that requires grounds for a divorce other than irreconcilable differences. They agree to enter into a public argument at a food court in their local shopping mall. In front of dozens of people, Monty calls Sarah a prostitute and strikes her across the face. Will Sarah have grounds for a divorce?

    (A) Yes, because Monty hit her.
    (B) Yes, because Monty falsely accused her of a crime.
    (C) No, because the actions do not meet the standards to permit a divorce.
    (D) No, because, due to the parties' collusion, no actual cruelty took place that would constitute grounds for divorce.

Questions 19–20 refer to the following fact pattern.

Kelly is the single mother of two children, Annette, who is nine years old and Annabelle, who is seven. For over ten years, Kelly has battled alcoholism. She has entered rehab facilities on several occasions, but, until recently, she has never succeeded in staying clean and sober for more than a few months.

Eighteen months ago, the state removed Annette and Annabelle from Kelly's care, arguing that Kelly was drinking heavily and had left the two small girls alone in the house on several occasions while she went out to a bar, drinking. Since that time, Annette and Annabelle have been living together with a foster family, a setting in which they have flourished. Their grades have gone up, they have been playing sports, their health has improved, and they profess to be quite happy.

19. Assume for the purposes of this question only that Kelly entered a rehabilitation facility immediately upon losing her children to the state. She has been clean and sober for the full eighteen months, and the rehab counselors predict that she will continue not to drink. Kelly has been attending AA meetings on a daily basis and feels confident that she is ready to take care of Annabelle and Annette. She is now petitioning to have them returned to her. The foster parents wish to adopt Annabelle and Annette and are opposing Kelly's petition.

    As her attorney, you should advise Kelly that

    (A) She is likely to regain custody of Annette and Annabelle because she is their natural mother.
    (B) She is likely to regain custody of Annette and Annabelle if, and only if, they say that they want to return and live with her. Otherwise, the foster parents will be allowed to adopt the girls.
    (C) She is unlikely to regain custody of Annette and Annabelle because of her history of alcoholism, and custody will therefore go to the foster parents.
    (D) She is unlikely to regain custody of Annette and Annabelle because they are flourishing in the foster home.

    BIC

20. Assume for the purposes of this question only that the children are returned to Kelly. After caring for them successfully for a year, Kelly learns that she has a slowly progressing form of multiple sclerosis. The doctors predict that Kelly will have difficulty walking within a few years but that she will otherwise remain fully functioning.

Hearing of Kelly's condition, the foster parents reenter the picture. They petition the court to allow them to adopt Annabelle and Annette. As Kelly's attorney you should advise her that

(A) She will likely retain custody of her daughters as long as she does not deteriorate beyond the need for crutches.
(B) She will likely retain custody of her daughters until her death or complete physical incapacity.
(C) She will likely lose custody immediately to the foster parents, who are both able-bodied.
(D) She will likely lose custody immediately to the foster parents, because her multiple sclerosis combined with her history of alcoholism make her less than an ideal parent.

Questions 21–22 refer to the following fact pattern.

Sandra and Marian have lived together for six years as roommates and best friends, but not as domestic partners. During that time, Sandra, as a single mother, has adopted two children, Emily and Teddy. Emily is now four-years old, and Teddy is two. Although it was officially Sandra who adopted the children, the two women agreed from the outset that Marian would participate heavily in raising the children. In fact, Sandra works full-time as a secretary, and it is Marian who usually cares for the children during the day.

21. Assume for the purposes of this question only that Sandra and Marian get into a big fight, and Marian moves out of the apartment they have shared. She now petitions the court for the right to visit Emily and Teddy. Is her petition likely to be granted?

(A) No, because she is not officially their parent, and there is no legal basis for visitation.
(B) No, because Sandra is entitled to make decisions about the children's welfare.
(C) Yes, because she has essentially been another parent to them for their entire lives.
(D) Yes, because it would be in Emily and Teddy's best interests.

22. Assume for the purposes of this question only that Sandra and Marian were romantically involved and that Emily and Teddy are the biological children of Sandra and an anonymous sperm donor. Assume also that Sandra gave birth to the children with the expectation that Marian would serve as a second parent to the children and that Marian wanted the same.

If Sandra and Marian break up, will Marian have a right to joint custody?

(A) Yes, because she is their mother just as much as Sandra is.
(B) Yes, if she has been the "stay-at-home" parent.
(C) No, because she has no biological connection to the children.
(D) No, because she is a lesbian and is not the biological parent of the children.

23. Which is the following statements is true with regards to the responsibility to pay child support after a divorce?

~~I.~~ Only the father must pay child support.

~~II.~~ The non-custodial parent must support the children because the custodial parent is caring for them.

III. The parents should divide support for the children equally.

(A) I only.
(B) II only.
(C) III only.
(D) None of the above.

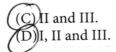

Questions 24–25 refer to the following fact pattern.

John and Molly have been married for sixteen years. During that time, John has built a substantial law practice and is now a senior partner at one of his city's top law firms. Molly has given birth to and cared full-time for the couple's three children, Katie, Maggie, and John, Jr.

24. John and Molly have now decided to obtain a divorce. Which of the following statements is most likely to be true?

I. Molly will be entitled to an equitable distribution of the couple's assets, including a share of John's law firm partnership.

II. John will be required to pay child support for the three children.

III. Molly may prevent John from seeing the children alone if the divorce is because he has been physically abusive to them.

IV. Molly will definitely be awarded the family home.

(A) All of the above.
(B) II, III and IV.
(C) II and III.
(D) I, II and III.

25. Will Molly be required to work outside the home after the divorce?

(A) No, not until the youngest child is in college.

(B) Yes, but only on a "mother's schedule" so that she can continue to care for the children outside of school hours.

(C) Probably not, but the court will take into account both the children's schedule and the burden to John to pay alimony.

(D) Yes, because it will be too much of a burden on John to set up a new home for himself and also to continue to support Molly and the kids.

1. (A)

All states require marriage licenses, and, although marriage is a fundamental right under the Constitution, states may set requirements for exercising that right. However, many states consider a marriage valid even in the absence of a license rather than requirements. Therefore, if Theresa and Henry lived in such a state, their marriage could be valid because (1) Theresa believed that the couple had a valid marriage license and was therefore acting in good faith, and (2) all other legal requirements were met. Note that (D) is incorrect because the state of mind of the Justice of the Peace would not be relevant in this situation.

2. (C)

The marriage will be valid in both State X and State Y because, even though State Y requires people to be 18 to be legally married, under the Full Faith and Credit Clause, states will recognize marriages that are legal in other states. Therefore, because the marriage is valid in State X, State Y will recognize the marriage. Note that (B) is incorrect because the couple's moving to State Y will not invalidate the marriage in State X. Answer choice (D) is incorrect because parental consent was not an issue in the question.

3. (D)

Here, Theresa's parents' threat was sufficient to overcome Henry's will and thus he is likely entitled to an annulment.

4. (C)

To answer this question, you would have to understand the difference between void marriages and voidable marriages. A voidable marriage is generally one that qualifies for annulment. Although a voidable marriage may be voided as of the date it began, it does not *have* to be voided. On the other hand, a void marriage is one where there is a strong public policy reason or impediment to a valid marriage, such as incest or bigamy. Therefore (A) and (B) must be incorrect, because both of them refer to the marriage as being voidable, whereas this marriage would be void because of the incest. Similarly, (D) is incorrect because it refers to the marriage as voidable. Only (C) correctly states that a bigamist marriage would be void *ab initio*.

5. (A)

Common law marriage is still recognized in several states. Note that, in this question, Allison and Bob meet the requirements most states would have for common law marriages. Also note that (B) is incorrect because the marriage would at least be recognized in other states that recognize common law marriages, if not in states that did not recognize common law marriage. (C) and (D) are clearly incorrect because common law marriages arise where the proper formalities have not been observed.

6. (A)

Henrietta clearly has grounds for divorce. Failure to engage in sexual relations is usually grounds for divorce. Note that Henrietta probably also has grounds for annulment because Gary seems to have misled Henrietta. (Henrietta can probably assert fraud as an essential aspect of marriage because Gary did not tell her that he was impotent or had a terminal illness). (B) and (C) are therefore incorrect. (D) is incorrect because, while the marriage was voidable due to Gary's apparent fraud, it would not be void. A void marriage would usually be one involving incest or bigamy.

7. (A)

Henrietta may no longer be able to rely on the impotence as the basis for an annulment, because she has now told Gary that the impotence did not matter. Similarly, Gary's illness will not be grounds for annulment in any case. Therefore, Henrietta probably cannot get an annulment at this point. Therefore, Henrietta's best course of action may be to seek a divorce. Note that (B) is incorrect because misrepresentations as to physical health are generally not grounds for an annulment. (D) is incorrect because, while the divorce may not be finalized for some time, Henrietta may certainly file for divorce at any time.

8. (B)

A promise to engage in sexual relations during marriage need not be express. (D) is therefore incorrect. In fact, it is generally assumed that married couples will engage in sexual relations. Therefore, because Gary did not engage in sexual relations with her, Henrietta can probably annul the marriage. Note that actual impotence (an inability to engage in sexual relations, as opposed to a lack of desire to do so) is not required. (C) is therefore incorrect.

9. (D)

While some states do have residency requirements before a spouse can initiate a divorce there, Carter has probably lived in Blackacre long enough to meet any such requirements. Therefore, Blackacre would probably have jurisdiction over the divorce. Note that the fact that the marriage originally occurred in Whiteacre is immaterial. Under the Full Faith and Credit Clause, each state must recognize the marriage and divorce decrees of every other state. Therefore, although Carter and Dolly were married in Whiteacre, the divorce need not occur in Whiteacre. (B) is incorrect because all states now recognize no-fault divorce. In most states, consent of both parties is not required to obtain a no-fault divorce.

10. (C)

In making custody determinations, courts generally consider only the best interests of the child. Note that the court will not be entitled to exercise its own discretion and take into account any factor it thinks is important; for example, courts may not consider the race of the parents and/or child in making custody determinations. In many states, it is unconstitutional to take into account the gender of the parent who is petitioning for custody. Note that (B) is incorrect because it is immaterial who is at fault in causing the divorce in deciding child custody issues. Similarly, (A) is incorrect because the wealthier parent will not automatically obtain custody. Indeed, it is for this very reason that child support is in place, so that a child may live with the parent who will protect that child's best interests, rather than with the wealthier parent. In other words, child support protects the child financially regardless of the income of the custodial parent.

11. (A)

In awarding alimony, a court will analyze the earning capacity of both spouses. If Larry earns much more than Sally, Sally will probably be entitled to alimony. Note that alimony is no longer gender-based; therefore, if Sally's earning capacity were higher than Larry's, Larry could be entitled to alimony. (D) is therefore incorrect. (B) is incorrect because, while Sally may very well have an equitable investment in Larry's education, that will not be the best argument for her to receive permanent alimony. Rather, it may be a good argument for her to receive some portion of the marital assets through an equitable distribution scheme. (C) is incorrect because alimony is not related to fault in divorce. While in many states adultery was once grounds for alimony to the adulterous spouse, most have done away with such requirements.

12. (C)

The purpose of rehabilitative alimony is to help a spouse develop means to support him or herself. Rehabilitative alimony will continue for as long as the court feels it is necessary. Note that rehabilitative alimony is the prevailing type in many states. (A) is incorrect because Kelly's investment in Larry's education would go to her right to an equitable distribution of the marital assets, not her right to rehabilitative alimony. (B) is incorrect because determination of the party responsible or at fault in the divorce does not enter into alimony considerations. While in many states adultery was once grounds for alimony to the adulterous spouse, most have done away with such requirements. (D) is incorrect because education is not an entitlement in divorce.

13. (C)

While in some states a professional license may be subject to equitable distribution, in most states it is not. In the states that do not allow such a license to be distributed, it is considered to be personal to the person who actually earned the license or degree. (A) and (B) are incorrect because these represent the minority view. (D) is incorrect because some states do allow for a professional license or degree to be distributed through an equitable distribution scheme.

14. (B)

Regardless of the financial status of the parties, a non-custodial parent generally will be required to pay child support, usually based on an income calculation. (A) is incorrect because, unless a child is somehow incapacitated and cannot support himself, a state will generally allow a non-custodial parent to cease paying child support when a child comes of age. (C) is incorrect because in most states today, the death of a non-custodial parent does terminate the allegation to pay child support. Note, however, that under the Uniform Marriage and Divorce Act, where a parent paying child support dies, the estate of that parent will continue to pay child support after the parent's death. (D) is incorrect because a child who is self-sufficient may still be entitled to child support. However, it is important to note that, in cases where children have unilaterally decided to live apart from their parents, this has in some cases been the basis for termination of a parent's obligation to pay child support.

15. (C)

Misrepresentations as to one's health are generally not grounds for annulment. However, (A), (B) and (D) are all incorrect because misrepresentation before marriage as to the desire to have children, as to criminal records, and as to extreme political beliefs may be grounds for annulment.

16. (B)

In order to obtain a divorce in a foreign country, generally both spouses must be aware of the divorce proceeding. However, (A) is incorrect because if both spouses went to Alberta and requested a divorce under the divorce laws in effect there, the United States would probably recognize such a divorce. (C) is incorrect because, under the Full Faith and Credit Clause, states will recognize the marriage and divorce decrees of other states. (D) is incorrect because the failure to recite the satisfaction of the residency requirement will not be material as long as that requirement was actually met.

17. (D)

Mental cruelty is a very broad standard, and it may include frequent insults, refusal to engage in sexual relations, frequent criticism and physical abuse. Therefore, all of Monty's actions may satisfy the grounds of cruelty.

18. (D)

In states that allow divorce to be filed on fault grounds, the parties cannot collude in order to create such grounds for divorce. Here, Monty and Sara entered into an agreement that Monty would be cruel to Sara. Therefore, because Sara consented to the cruelty and colluded with Monty to create grounds for divorce, Sara may not assert Monty's cruelty in the shopping mall in filing for divorce. (C) is incorrect because, had Sara not colluded with Monty, Monty's actions might rise to level necessary for Sara to file for divorce on the basis of cruelty, particularly if Monty's actions were not limited to this one occasion. (A) and (B) are incorrect because his physical abuse and his accusations were manufactured and were not genuine.

19. (A)

Here, Kelly has demonstrated that she can be a responsible member of society. Therefore, because there is a strong presumption that a natural parent will have custody of her own children, Kelly will probably regain custody of Annette and Annabelle. (C) is incorrect because Annette and Annabelle's wishes will not be material when there is a fit natural parent who can care for them. (D) is incorrect because courts do take into account the present status of the natural parents and not only their history of unfitness. (B) is incorrect because, although they may be flourishing in the foster home, a natural parent will presumably recover custody of her own children where she is fit to do so.

20. (B)

Even if Kelly is becoming physically incapacitated, the court is not likely to remove the children from her care unless the incapacity reaches such a stage that Kelly genuinely cannot care for the children. (A) is therefore incorrect because, even if Kelly were to deteriorate beyond the need for crutches, she could probably still care for Annabelle and Annette. (C) and (D) are also incorrect, because the presumption will be that the children will remain with Kelly until her incapacity reaches such a stage that she cannot care for them. At that point, the foster parents might have a case for the children to be returned to their care, but only if there are no blood relatives who can take over the care for Annabelle and Annette.

21. (B)

Although Marian has played a major role in Emily and Teddy's life, the court is not likely to grant her visitation. Parents (in this case, Sandra) are considered to be allowed, constitutionally, to make decisions for their children. It has even been held that grandparents may not participate in the lives of their grandchildren if the parent does not wish them to. (A) is incorrect because there may be some legal basis for visitation if the court were to find that a lack of Marian's visitation would be harmful to the children. (C) is incorrect because she lacks parental status. In similar cases, even people who have acted as parents may not be granted visitation. (D) is incorrect because, while visits from Marian may be Emily and Teddy's best interests, Marian will only be allowed to visit them again if Sandra wishes, or if her inability to visit Emily and Teddy would be extremely harmful to the children.

22. (A)

While A is probably the best answer, this question is difficult to answer, because different courts take different considerations into account. (C) is certain incorrect, because, in the case of adoptive parents, there is no biological connection to the children, and adoptive parents are routinely granted joint custody. (D) is incorrect because, while some courts do take sexual orientation into account in making custody decisions, not all courts do. (B) is incorrect because joint custody is often granted to a parent who has not stayed at home with the children. Therefore, although it will probably be an uphill battle for Marian because she does not have any legal connection to the children, (A) is probably the best answer of the four.

23. (D)

I is clearly wrong, because a non-custodial parent, regardless of gender, generally must pay child support. II is clearly incorrect because if a custodial parent does have some financial obligation to support the children. III is incorrect, because financial support generally is not divided equally, but rather based on the ability of the parents to pay. (D) is therefore the correct answer.

24. (D)

I is likely to be correct. Molly will be entitled to an equitable distribution of the couple's assets, and John's law firm partnership may very well be a marital asset. II is a correct statement because John will certainly be required to pay child support for his children. III is likely to be correct. John will probably be allowed to see the children, but he may have to have supervised visitations. Only in very rare cases does the court refuse to allow a biological parent to see his children at all. IV is not correct. The custodial mother is not necessarily entitled to the family home. Rather, the family home will be a marital asset that will be awarded pursuant to an equitable distribution scheme in most states. Therefore, (D) is the correct answer.

25. (C)

Again, this question is difficult to answer, because the court will take into account each family's particular circumstances. (A) is probably incorrect, however, because it is unlikely that John will be required to support Molly and the children for the number of years it would take for their youngest child to enter college. (B) is probably incorrect, because while this is certainly a possibility that Molly and John can agree to, a court will be reluctant to issue such an order. (D) is probably incorrect because John would almost certainly have to pay alimony for some period of time. Therefore, while this question is difficult to answer, (C) is probably the best answer.

ESSAY QUESTIONS

Questions 1–4 refer to the following fact pattern.

Kathleen and John Smith are the parents of ten-year-old Suzy and eight-year-old Jack. Kathleen and John are currently seeking a divorce. John's parents, Douglas and Barbara Smith, are very involved in the lives of the children, and, up until the time of the divorce, commonly saw the children at least once a week.

Kathleen and John's divorce is quite contentious. Kathleen does not want to return to work, believing that a mother's place is in the home with her children. She has been a stay-at-home mom since the birth of her first child. John has worked at an excellent, well-paying job for this time period and has adequately supported the family. John, however, believes that he should not have to pay alimony because the children are old enough so that they do not require a full-time stay-at-home parent. He also points out that Kathleen holds a law degree from Harvard Law School, and that he supported her fully while she attended Harvard Law School and earned the degree. He also paid her tuition. Kathleen practiced law for four years before the birth of their first child. John is seeking two things in the divorce: (i) joint custody of the children and (ii) equitable distribution of the marital assets, including some "pay back" for helping Kathleen earn her law degree.

Douglas and Barbara Smith seek weekly visitation with their grandchildren. Kathleen opposes such visitation, at least during the dates that the children are residing with her.

1. Must Kathleen return to work? If she does not, must John pay her alimony?

2. Is joint custody appropriate in this situation?

3. Is John entitled to a share of Kathleen's law degree?

4. Are Douglas and Barbara Smith entitled to visitation against Kathleen's wishes?

Questions 5–7 refer to the following fact pattern.

Albert and Harry are two gay men who live in the state of Utopia. They met approximately five years ago and have been dating exclusively ever since. A year ago, Albert and Harry moved in together and are now living in Harry's home, which he owns.

5. Assume for the purposes of this question only that the town where Albert and Harry live recently passed an ordinance prohibiting people who are not "immediate family" from living together. Would this ordinance affect Albert and Harry's living arrangement?

6. Assume for the purposes of this question only that Albert and Harry decide to formalize their relationship. What options would be available to them and where?

7. Assume for the purposes of this question only that Albert and Harry wish to become parents. What options are available to them legally?

8. Describe a putative marriage and when such a marriage is enforceable.

9. Describe a common law marriage.

10. Describe the concept of annulment.

Questions 11–12 refer to the following fact pattern.

You are a lawyer in the state of Blackacre. Anna and Scott come to you for legal advice. Anna and Scott are planning to get married in one month's time. Because Anna has significant assets, which she inherited from her grandmother, Anna and Scott wish to enter into a prenuptial agreement.

11. What advice would you give Anna and Scott about what the agreement should contain and what each of their rights under such an agreement would be?

12. Assume for the purposes of this question only that Anna and Scott are already married when they come to you. Fifty years ago, her father founded a chain of dry cleaners, which has been incredibly successful. The chain is now worth approximately $50,000,000. Anna has inherited the business from her father, and she is concerned that she protect this asset and keep it within her family. While Anna and Scott are still happily married, she is concerned that, if that should change in the future, Scott would have access to the asset of the dry cleaning business. What legal advice would you give her?

13. Frances and Sean are a married couple. For years, Frances and Sean have struggled with infertility. Finally, they have acknowledged that Frances will not be able to achieve a successful pregnancy. Therefore, they have decided to go through an agency and use a surrogate mother to have a child for them. The surrogate would be impregnated with Sean's sperm. Therefore, the child would be biologically Sean's, but not biologically related to Frances.

Frances and Sean seek your legal advice as to what issues may arise in such an arrangement. What advice should you give them?

Questions 14–17 refer to the following fact pattern.

Twenty years ago, Jessica and Michael went to Las Vegas and got married. At the time, they were residents of the State of Whiteacre. In Las Vegas, they obtained a Nevada marriage license. On the application for the license, both Michael and Jessica stated that they had never before been married. The marriage ceremony was conducted by an Elvis impersonator who was wearing a white leather suit and blue suede shoes. Last week, Jessica learned that Michael has been living a double life. He has been married to a woman in another city for the past thirty years. Jessica is devastated. She wants to whether her marriage can possibly be valid, or whether she has never legally been married. She also wants to know whether their three children, Sue, Kathy, and Elizabeth are legitimate or illegitimate in this situation.

14. Is Jessica and Michael's *putative* marriage a legitimate marriage? What legal options are available to Jessica? *annulment or treat like divorce*

15. Assume for the purposes of this question only that Michael now wishes to seek a divorce from the woman in the other city. If he does so, will the marriage between Jessica and Michael be valid, or will they have to remarry? *no. yes.*

16. Assume for the purposes of this question only that Michael wishes to remain married to the woman in the other city but now wishes to end his "marriage" with Jessica. What is a proper means for ending the relationship? *walk away annulment? divide prop spousal support b/c putative. good faith*

17. Are Sue, Kathy, and Elizabeth legitimate? Explain your answer.

18. What are the key issues around which most divorces now resolve? Explain your answer.

19. Distinguish the types of fault-based divorce from no-fault grounds.

Questions 20–22 refer to the following fact pattern.

Jennifer and Glen, two celebrities, are engaged to be married. Unfortunately, they must await the finalization of Jennifer's divorce before they can marry. Jennifer, an actress and singer, was married for about ten months to her manager, Christian. She then filed for divorce. While Christian did not contest the divorce, the property settlement was contested, and their divorce has therefore taken over a year.

20. Assume for the purposes of this question only that the state in which Jennifer and Glen reside has the following statute in effect:

   "Couple who wish to marry must certify that they are free to do so. Couples are not free to marry if (a) they have been divorced within the last year or (b) they are siblings, parent/child, grandparent/grandchild, aunt/nephew, uncle/niece, or first cousins."

   Assume also for the purposes of this question only that yesterday, the court granted Jennifer a divorce from Christian.

   Jennifer and Glen wish to get married next month. However, they are concerned that the state statute will prevent them from doing so. How would you advise them and why?

21. Assume for the purposes of this question only that Jennifer and Christian were legally divorced last week and that Jennifer and Glen married last night. Assume also that Jennifer and Christian's divorce only took one month to go through. Finally, assume that no "cooling off" statute exists in this jurisdiction.

   Jennifer learned yesterday that she is 14 weeks pregnant. Because she and Glen have always used birth control, and because of the timing of the pregnancy, she is fairly certain that Christian is the biological father.

   Who will be the baby's legal father, and why?

22. Explain the concept of equitable distribution and the public policy reasons behind it.

23. Describe the differences between prenuptial and post-nuptial agreements and discuss the enforceability issues of each.

Questions 24–25 refer to the following fact pattern.

Abigail, a new client, comes to see you to discuss her concerns that her parental rights may be terminated. She is the natural mother of two children, Marianne, age three, and William, age seven. She desperately wants to keep her children, but she is genuinely concerned that they may be taken from her.

24. On what bases may her parental rights be terminated without her consent?

25. If Abigail's parental rights are validly terminated, who will have standing to adopt Marianne and William?

1. Must Kathleen return to work? If she does not, must John pay her alimony?

In order to answer this question, it will be important to know the time frame we are talking about. Kathleen may very well be required to return to work at some point, but the point at which she will have to return will likely be a negotiation point between the parties in the divorce and the property settlement. After all, according to the fact pattern, Kathleen has not been in the work force for at least ten years. Although she holds a degree from an excellent law school and has some work experience (four years' worth), she does not have any legal or other work experience within the last ten years, a fact which will perhaps make it difficult for her to find work. She may need additional training and education to bring her up to speed to enter today's work force.

In making a decision about alimony, the court will certainly take into account the terms of the property settlement and distribution. The public policy reason behind alimony is to provide support for people who cannot support themselves. If Kathleen's property settlement is such that she can support herself based on the assets she receives, she is less likely to receive any or a large amount of alimony.

Therefore, based on Kathleen's long absence from the work force and the fact that theirs was a long-term marriage, the court will probably require John to pay at least rehabilitative alimony for some period of time, at least until Kathleen can make arrangements for the children and prepare herself to enter the work force. It is unlikely, however, that John will be required to pay permanent alimony or to support Kathleen indefinitely or until or unless she remarries.

2. Is joint custody appropriate in this situation?

Joint custody may well be appropriate in this situation. In some states, joint custody is awarded unless there is some reason not to do so. In other states, whether or not joint custody is awarded depends on what the court determines will be in the best interests of the children.

In this fact pattern, there is nothing to suggest that John is anything other than a fit, caring parent. If he desires joint custody and can demonstrate to the court that he can make beneficial arrangements for the children while he works, the court may well grant his request. Because courts no longer determine custody based on the gender of the petitioning parent, the fact that John is a man should not work against him, as it might have in the past. On the other hand, Kathleen may be able to make a case that, because she has been the children's primary caretaker, she should retain primary custody. This argument would probably hold more weight with many courts, however, if the children were younger. Indeed, the children are verging on the age where they may have some say in the custody arrangement.

Based on the facts, John will likely have a case for joint custody.

3. Is John entitled to a share of Kathleen's law degree?

While John may not be entitled to a "share" of the degree, per se, whether or not he can be compensated for having contributed to her earning of the degree will probably depend on the state he lives in. In some states, the degree will be considered to be marital property and will be "distributed" in a property settlement under equitable distribution doctrine. In other words, in light of the fact that Kathleen has the degree, from which John will now derive no benefit, John will receive some other asset of value. However, in most states, the degree is considered to be the product of its holder's hard work and is therefore not considered to be property in the traditional sense. If John and Kathleen live in one of the majority states, therefore, John will probably receive nothing in an equitable distribution scenario.

4. Are Douglas and Barbara Smith entitled to visitation against Kathleen's wishes?

Until recently, Douglas and Barbara Smith would have stood a good chance of prevailing in their request for visitation with Suzy and Jack. Many courts would have applied the "best interests of the child" test in determining whether Douglas and Barbara should visit the children, even over Kathleen's objection. Given the fact that, prior to the divorce, the grandparents were very involved in the lives of the children and saw them at least weekly, it seems reasonable to assume that many judges would have felt it to be in the best interests of these school-aged children to have continued contact with their grandparents. Other courts might have employed a stricter standard and examined whether separation from their grandparents would be harmful to Jack and Suzy. Under this analysis, the grandparents may or may not have prevailed, depending on what evidence the court heard about the short and long-term effects on the children.

However, assuming that Douglas and Barbara have brought their action after the year 2000, they may lose their petition to visit the children while they are in Kathleen's care. In the very similar case of *Troxel v. Granville*, the Supreme Court reiterated that fit parents have a fundamental right to control who visits with their children, even if the proposed visitors are blood relatives (other than the parents themselves). 530 U.S. 57 (2000). In that case, a state statute provided that anyone could visit children if that visitation was in the best interests of the child. The Supreme Court struck down the statute in favor of a mother who wanted to keep her deceased husband's parents from visiting frequently with her children. Because it will be difficult for Douglas and Barbara to distinguish their petition from that of the grandparents in *Troxel*, they are unlikely to prevail.

5. Assume for the purposes of this question only that the town where Albert and Harry live recently passed an ordinance prohibiting people who are not "immediate family" from living together. Would this ordinance affect Albert and Harry's living arrangement?

Yes, the ordinance probably would affect Albert and Harry's living arrangement. In *Moore v. City of E. Cleveland*, the Supreme Court articulated the fundamental right of related people to live together. However, this right has not been extended to unrelated people. One frequently tested issue is whether long-term domestic partnerships are protected under the Constitution. Because the fundamental right only applies to people who are related by blood, marriage, or adoption, the consistent answer to this question is that such partnerships are not protected in areas that do not recognize them legally.

Albert and Harry may want to examine whether Harry, as a property owner, can have Albert as a long-term guest or tenant under the statute or whether he can convey a portion of the home to Albert so that Albert would be able to assert ownership/property rights.

6. Assume for the purposes of this question only that Albert and Harry decide to formalize their relationship. What options would be available to them and where?

As of the time of this writing, Albert and Harry would do best to formalize their relationship by marrying in the state of Massachusetts or by moving to a state that recognizes civil unions or domestic partnerships. In civil union and domestic partnership states homosexual couples may enter into these marriage-like commitments, which involve licenses, official ceremonies, and all the benefits of traditional marriage (pension, social welfare benefits, etc.). Albert and Harry should note, however, that, if they decide to end the relationship, they will have to do so formally through the state's court system.

7. Assume for the purposes of this question only that Albert and Harry wish to become parents. What options are available to them legally?

Some states now allow homosexual couples to adopt children, and many allow homosexuals who are single to do so. Therefore, adoption may be one option for Albert and Harry. Of course, they may attempt to adopt domestically through an attorney or an agency, or they may try to adopt internationally. They may encounter difficulty in either situation due to cultural prejudices, however, and so biological parenthood may make more sense for them.

If they wish to become biological parents, two options are available to them. First, they may find a woman willing to be inseminated with either Albert or Harry's sperm who will carry the baby to term. Such a situation is called surrogacy. In this type of arrangement, the surrogate would then relinquish the baby to Albert and Harry upon its birth. If Albert and Harry want to minimize the chances that the surrogate would be able to change her mind and keep the baby, they might want to consider egg donation. In this situation, a woman would donate an egg to be fertilized with Albert or Harry's sperm. The resulting embryo would then be implanted in the surrogate's uterus but would not be biologically related to her.

Upon the birth of such a baby, Albert and Harry would want to look into the laws of their state to determine whether the man who did not provide the sperm—i.e., the one that is not biologically related—may adopt the child.

The other option that Albert and Harry may want to consider is whether they would like to co-parent with a woman who would carry their child. In such a case, the woman would remain involved in the child's life but would, again, be inseminated with Albert or Harry's sperm.

8. Describe a putative marriage and when such a marriage is enforceable.

A putative marriage may exist where one person has been living with one of the opposite sex in a genuine belief that the two are married, even though they are not. Such a marriage may arise where, *ab initio*, there was some legal impediment to the marriage—for example, a previous marriage, a previously unknown blood relationship, or some other impediment—of which the innocent spouse was unaware.

Such a relationship is not a valid marriage and is not enforceable as one. However, because the innocent party had a good faith belief that s/he was married, s/he may be entitled to compensation and/or benefits upon discovery of the defect and termination of the relationship, just as s/he would be in the case of a divorce in a legitimate marriage.

9. Describe a common law marriage.

A common law marriage may arise in some states where the "spouses" have not complied with the statutory formalities—e.g., obtainment of a marriage license, participation in a marriage ceremony—required for marriage in those states. In the case of common law marriage, the "spouses" have declared their commitment and consent to be married. In most states, they must also live together and publicly hold themselves out to be husband and wife. Interestingly, although most people believe that, in order to be married under the common law, two people must live together for a certain period of time, such is not actually the case in most states. Therefore, just as spouses who are married under conventional, statutorily approved means are married upon compliance with statutory formalities, so too are spouses who marry under the common law married once they have engaged in the behavior necessary under the common law.

In states that recognize common law marriage, it is a completely legitimate form of marriage. This means that, if the parties wish to end the relationship, they must do so through conventional means, i.e., divorce or annulment. If the parties divorce, the court will employ the usual means to divide their assets.

Furthermore, children of a common law marriage are legitimate because their parents are legally married. Both parents in such a situation would have a right to visitation and a duty to support the children in the case of a divorce.

Note that a person may not enter into a common law marriage if any of the standard impediments to marriage exist. Therefore, a relationship will not be a common law marriage if it is incestuous or bigamous or if both parties have not consented to the marriage.

10. Describe the concept of annulment.

An annulment is one way through which people who have married may dissolve the marriage. However, an annulment is only appropriate in a situation in which the marriage is void or voidable. In other words, in granting an annulment, the court is actually stating that the parties were never legally married because of some impediment to their marriage or because the original agreement to marry was invalid.

Therefore, in deciding whether to grant an annulment, a court will look to see whether the marriage was void because it was incestuous or bigamous. It will also look to see whether the parties were capable of entering into a marriage and competent to do so. Of course, it will invalidate a marriage where one of the parties was the victim of fraud or duress in entering into the marriage. However, a court usually will not annul a marriage where a fraudulent statement, if known, would not have prevented the innocent spouse from entering into the marriage or goes to a matter non-essential to the marital relationship.

Note that, in most states, if children were born of a marriage before it was annulled, these children will be considered to be legitimate. Note also that many states require an aggrieved party to bring an action for annulment within some statutorily prescribed period of time.

11. What advice would you give Anna and Scott about what the agreement should contain and what each of their rights under such an agreement would be?

Anna and Scott are contemplating the creation of a prenuptial (or antenuptial) agreement. The first thing that Anna and Scott should realize is that such an agreement would only go into effect in the event that they were to divorce or one person were to die. Second, the couple should understand that they should be very sure about the contents of the agreement, as most courts will consider such an agreement to be valid and enforceable. Prenuptial agreements are contracts, and, as long as they are executed with proper contractual formalities, typical contract law will control their enforceability. Therefore, Anna and Scott must make their agreement in good faith, and they must make sure that the terms of the agreement are fair and reasonable.

Anna and Scott may choose to include several different types of provisions in their prenuptial agreement. First, and most obviously, the agreement should contain a clause stating that Scott may not reach Anna's pre-marital assets in the event of a divorce. Note that, if Scott and Anna do not live in an equitable distribution or community property state, this clause will be particularly important, because such a state will not recognize separate property. This clause would therefore be instrumental in determining the distribution of all assets owned by the parties.

Second, Anna and Scott may also contract for the distribution of their joint marital assets. Again, if the way in which they decide that they will divide their assets is reasonable, most courts will comply with the terms of the prenuptial agreement in distributing the assets.

Third, Anna and Scott may contract as to the terms of any alimony arrangement. This clause could contain provisions about who will be required to pay alimony to whom, in what amount, and for how long. Again, a court will typically enforce such a provision unless it is unfair in some way.

Fourth, Anna and Scott may make provisions for child custody and support for their future children. This clause, however, may be the least enforceable. When deciding custody and support issues, even in the case of prenuptial agreements, courts typically look at the best interests of the children. Therefore, the court will only enforce any support/custody provision if it is convinced that the terms of such a clause are in the best interests of Anna and Scott's future children.

12. **Assume for the purposes of this question only that Anna and Scott do not have a pre-nuptial agreement. While Anna and Scott are still happily married, she is concerned that, if that should change in the future, Scott would have access to the asset of the dry cleaning business. What legal advice would you give her?**

In this case, the type of jurisdiction that Anna and Scott live in will be instrumental. If they live in a community property equitable distribution state, Scott will not have access to the asset of the dry cleaning business if he and Anna divorce. This is because equitable distribution and community property states treat inherited property as separate property that is not subject to equitable distribution. Therefore, Anna would retain ownership of the dry cleaning business.

If Anna and Scott do not live in an equitable distribution or community property state, however, they will want to draft a post-nuptial agreement. A post-nuptial agreement is very similar to a prenuptial agreement except that it is executed after the parties are already married. Like a prenuptial agreement, a post-nuptial agreement is generally enforceable. Anna and Scott should be able to agree in writing that, should they divorce, Scott will not have access to the asset of the dry cleaning business.

The most difficult part of drafting this agreement may be obtaining Scott's consent. Scott may be offended that, while he believes himself to be happily married to Anna, she sees the need for such an agreement. Furthermore, he may recognize that such an agreement will cut off any claim that he would otherwise have to the dry cleaning business. Therefore, part of the client counseling process with Anna should include a discussion of the impact that creation of such an agreement could have on her relationship with Scott.

13. **Frances and Sean seek your legal advice as to what issues may arise in such an arrangement. What advice should you give them?**

There has been a great deal of publicity about the issues surrounding surrogacy. There are several factors that Frances and Sean will want to consider.

First, Frances and Sean will want to draw up a contract with the surrogate in which the surrogate agrees to terminate her parental rights upon the baby's birth. Some courts find such clauses to be enforceable, although others do not. For this reason, Frances and Sean will also want to think carefully about the issues below.

Second, Frances will want to talk with her doctor about whether her own eggs could be retrieved and then inseminated with Sean's sperm. Should Frances and Sean use Frances' egg, the surrogate would then be only a gestational carrier and would not be biologically related to the baby, a fact that would work in favor of Frances and Sean should a dispute arise with the surrogate about custody of the baby, as they would be the biological parents.

Third, if Frances' eggs are not viable, Frances and Sean may want to consider using a donor egg that would be inseminated with Sean's sperm, then implanted in the uterus of the surrogate. Again, should they do so, the surrogate would then be only a gestational carrier and would not be biologically related to the baby, a fact that would work in favor of Frances and Sean should a dispute arise with the surrogate about custody of the baby.

Fourth, Frances and Sean will want to consider the physical and emotional health of the surrogate. If the surrogate is simply inseminated with Sean's sperm (i.e., her own egg is used), then she may pass on any genetic or inheritable conditions that run in her family. Even if a donor egg or Frances' egg is used, the surrogate may pass on sexually transmitted diseases to the baby. Emotionally, Frances and Sean will want to choose a stable surrogate who fully appreciates the impact that giving up the baby is likely to have on her. An emotionally stable surrogate is more likely to complete the surrogacy arrangement successfully than one with a history of psychological difficulties.

Fifth, Frances and Sean will want to consider working through an agency to find a suitable surrogate who meets the other criteria listed here. Most agencies have a screening process for surrogates and only use surrogates who are likely in all respects to comply with the terms of a surrogacy agreement.

Sixth, Frances and Sean will want to be careful about what form compensation to the surrogate will take. Most states have statutes that prohibit "baby selling." They will probably need to ensure that any payment to the surrogate is for her expenses and effort and not for the baby itself.

Fifth, Frances and Sean will want to look into the possibility of Frances' adopting the baby after its birth if her egg is not used (or, in some jurisdictions, even if it is, as she will not give birth to the baby).

14. Is Jessica and Michael's marriage a legitimate marriage? What legal options are available to Jessica?

Jessica and Michael's marriage was void *ab initio*, because Michael was already married at the time that he married Jessica. Bigamy is illegal in all U.S. jurisdictions. However, because Jessica did not know about Michael's other "wife," she had a good faith belief that they were actually married, and she is therefore a putative spouse.

Jessica therefore has several legal options. First, she may simply leave Michael. Because the marriage was a void one (because Michael was already married), there is no need for her to obtain a judicial declaration that the marriage is invalid.

Second, Jessica may seek an annulment on the basis of bigamy. The annulment will certainly be granted, given Michael's preexisting marriage. An annulment will simply be a judicial acknowledgement of the underlying fact that the marriage between the two was void.

Third, because this is a putative marriage and she is an innocent party, Jessica may treat this as the breakdown of a marriage. As such, she will certainly be entitled to claim a portion of the "marital" assets, and she may also be entitled to alimony or support.

15. **Assume for the purposes of this question only that Michael now wishes to seek a divorce from the woman in the other city. If he does so, will the marriage between Jessica and Michael be valid, or will they have to remarry?**

The answer to this question will depend on the laws of the state in which Jessica and Michael live. In some states, because Michael's bigamy rendered their marriage void *ab initio*, Jessica and Michael were never married at all. Therefore, in this type of state, once Michael's divorce from the other woman is final, Jessica and Michael would have follow all of the formalities required by their state (e.g., get a marriage license, have blood tests, attend a formal marriage ceremony, etc.) and actually marry each other again.

In other states, however, Michael and Jessica's marriage would be considered valid once Michael obtained a divorce from the other woman. Jessica clearly believed that she was married to Michael, and her good faith belief will probably save the marriage.

16. **Assume for the purposes of this question only that Michael wishes to remain married to the woman in the other city but now wishes to end his "marriage" with Jessica. What is a proper means for ending the relationship?**

The answer to this question is actually much the same as the answer to Question #14. Jessica and Michael's marriage was void *ab initio*, because Michael was already married at the time that he married Jessica.

Michael, like Jessica, therefore has several legal options. First, he may simply leave Jessica. Because the marriage was a void one (because Michael was already married), there is no need for him to obtain a judicial declaration that the marriage is invalid. Note also that most jurisdictions also provide for criminal sanctions for bigamy.

Second, Michael may seek an annulment on the basis of bigamy. The annulment will certainly be granted, given Michael's preexisting marriage. An annulment will simply be a judicial acknowledgement of the underlying fact that the marriage between the two was void.

However, unlike Jessica, Michael probably cannot treat this as a putative marriage. As the facts indicate that he has been living a double life, he presumably is not an innocent party in this situation. Therefore, he probably may not treat this as the breakdown of a marriage, and he probably will not be entitled to alimony or support from Jessica. However, in the interests of fairness, he probably can claim a portion of any assets he owns jointly with Jessica. Although he has been deluding her about their relationship for twenty years, most courts would not require him to relinquish all of his assets, as such an action would amount to punishment.

17. Are Sue, Kathy, and Elizabeth legitimate? Explain your answer.

Under the Uniform Marriage and Divorce Act, Sue, Kathy, and Elizabeth are probably legitimate. The recent American trend has been in favor of finding children to be legitimate whenever possible (probably because of the stigma that accompanies illegitimacy and because a child cannot control whether or not her parents were married at the time of her birth). Indeed, according to the Supreme Court, a state would have a heavy burden to prove that a law distinguishing between legitimate and illegitimate children was constitutional. Given the fact that Jessica and Michael have been engaged in some form of putative marriage and have held themselves out to be spouses, as well as the fact that the three girls were born during this "marriage," most states will consider them to be legitimate.

Legitimacy can be an advantage under some outdated laws, most of which have been repealed or declared unconstitutional. However, under such laws, illegitimate children sometimes could not inherit property, receive government benefits due them, or sue for the wrongful death of their parents. Therefore, Jessica will probably want to take action to have Sue, Kathy, and Elizabeth declared legitimate under the laws of the state in which they live.

18. What are the key issues around which most divorces now revolve? Explain your answer.

Most divorces now revolve around the issues of property division, child custody, alimony, and child support. Because all states now offer an alternative to fault-based divorce, many fewer divorces revolve around which party actually caused the breakdown of the marriage. Indeed, many couples no longer wish to air their dirty laundry and simply file for divorce on the basis of irretrievable breakdown of the marriage or irreconcilable differences, even where fault-based grounds for divorce may exist. Furthermore, most courts now employ a number of factors in making decisions related to a divorce, and the identity of the party at fault is a rather minor consideration in most cases.

Property division can be contentious because most courts now employ the concept of equitable distribution. Some spouses feel that such a doctrine is unfair, because, under equitable distribution, the court does not divide property equally (as in community property states), but rather equitably, taking into account each spouse's contribution to the marriage. Furthermore, spouses may conflict about what property is marital property and what property is separate.

Child custody is also typically a point of contention. Most states no longer presume that the mother will automatically obtain custody of the children. Therefore, establishing the terms of custody and visitation may take some negotiation.

Child support may be a point of contention, but it really should not be. Many states now have statutory calculations by which they determine how much child support a non-custodial parent must pay. Of course, all states require parents to support their children either by caring for them custodially, providing for them financially, or both.

Alimony may well be a point of contention. Many spouses may feel that they are entitled to alimony, but courts have gotten stricter in this respect. Before awarding alimony, most courts will take into account the length of the marriage, the ability of the payee spouse to support him/herself, and the length of time for which alimony is requested. Permanent alimony has become rarer, with most states favoring a form of rehabilitative alimony that will give a person to "get on his feet" and become self-supporting.

19. Distinguish the types of fault-based divorce from no-fault grounds.

There are several fault-based grounds for divorce, including adultery, cruelty, desertion, non-support, conviction for a serious crime, insanity, impotence, and habitual intoxication. Note that each state legislature has established different grounds for divorce. Earlier in our country's history, a spouse who wished to obtain a divorce had to establish valid grounds to do so. The fact that a marriage was simply unworkable would not suffice.

In recent years, however, most states have recognized the wisdom of establishing certain no-fault based grounds. These usually take the form of either "irreconcilable differences" or "irretrievable breakdown of the marriage." In some of these states, one spouse may simply declare that there is no chance that the marriage can succeed. In other states, both spouses must so declare. In any event, all states now allow some form of no-fault divorce, making it possible for people to divorce without establishment of the traditional grounds.

20. Jennifer and Glen wish to get married next month. However, they are concerned that the state statute will prevent them from doing so. How would you advise them and why?

You should probably advise Jennifer and Glen that the state statute may be enforceable, but that they do have grounds to attack it. Some states prohibit remarriage for a short period of time after a final divorce decree has been granted. These states want to give the divorcing spouses time to reconcile, should they so desire, and a little time to clear their heads before moving on directly into another marriage. Some states allow the party who did not file for divorce to remarry more quickly than the party who actually filed (in an effort to keep people from divorcing their spouses in order to marry others).

Most of the statutes that require a waiting period, however, limit the time before allowing remarriage to a few months. Here, the statute requires Jennifer to wait a year before she can remarry. Jennifer may therefore be able to challenge the statute on Constitutional grounds by asserting that the statute interferes with her fundamental right to marry. It will probably be difficult for the state to make an argument that it has a compelling state interest to keep recently divorced people from remarrying for an entire year. Therefore, should Jennifer sue to have the statute declared unconstitutional, she will probably win.

Unfortunately, the fact that the statute is probably unconstitutional does not help Jennifer and Glen with their immediate problem: the fact that Jennifer is now divorced and they want to marry. The office that issues marriage licenses will deny them a license because, as of this date, the statute is still in effect. A constitutional challenge may take some time. Therefore, Jennifer and Glen may want to travel to another state that does not require a waiting period and marry there. Under the Full Faith and Credit Clause, their home state should then recognize their marriage.

21. Who will be the baby's legal father, and why?

Now that Glen and Jennifer are married, under the laws of most states, Glen will be presumed to be the baby's legal father (assuming that Glen and Jennifer are still married when the baby is born). Most states presume that the mother's husband is the father of her baby. However, in most states, either the mother or the biological father may rebut this presumption by demonstrating that the mother's husband could not be the father of the child. This may be accomplished in a number of ways.

First, Glen and Christian could submit to blood tests which will conclusively determine who is the father of the child. These tests will not be performed, however, until after the child's birth.

Second, depending on whether she wants Glen to be declared the baby's legal father, Jennifer may submit an affidavit declaring that she had sexual intercourse with Christian around the time she became pregnant. She may also declare that she does not believe that Glen could be the father because she always used birth control with him. The court may then, based on this evidence, declare Christian to be the baby's father.

Third, Christian could declare himself to be the baby's father and endeavor to prove it in either of the above ways. However, he should note that the Supreme Court has said that he does not have an absolute right to do so absent Jennifer's joining in his paternity petition, because his petition could have a very negative effect on the marriage, and the state has an interest in protecting and preserving marriage. In other words, in some states, while Jennifer or Glen would be allowed to bring an action declaring Christian to be the true father of the baby, Christian could not independently bring such an action.

Both Christian and Glen should note that the legal father of Jennifer's baby will have an obligation to contribute to that baby's support.

22. Explain the concept of equitable distribution and the public policy reasons behind it.

In the case of a divorce, most states now divide the marital assets of a couple equitably (although not always equally, as community property states do). The marital assets are usually defined as assets acquired by a couple during a marriage and generally do not include inherited property, gifts made to one partner, property held by one partner before the marriage, or property received by one party after the parties have separated. Equitable distribution attempts to distribute property to each spouse in proportion to the contribution each spouse has made to the marriage, but does not rely on the financial contribution each has made. Indeed, a homemaker spouse or one who has supported the other emotionally and psychologically may well receive a large share of the marital assets, even where that spouse has made little or no financial contribution to the marriage. In other words, when equitably dividing a couple's assets, the court takes into account the different roles the spouses have played in the marriage and divides the assets in a way that fairly reflects the contributions each spouse has made. Because division of the assets is a reflection of the economic value of each spouse's various contributions, the court will rarely consider who was at fault in causing the events that led to divorce.

23. Describe the differences between prenuptial and post-nuptial agreements and discuss the enforceability issues of each.

A prenuptial, or antenuptial, agreement, is one in which, prior to the marriage, the spouses contract for the division of marital assets in the event of a divorce. A post-nuptial agreement is similar in all respects to an antenuptial agreement except that it is executed at some point after the spouses are already married. While most people think of these types of agreements only in the context of a marriage between a wealthy person and one of few assets, such is not the case. Both pre- and post-nuptial agreements are increasingly common in American family law.

Assuming that a pre- or post-nuptial agreement complies with contractual requirements and formalities, a court will show great deference to the contract between the parties and will generally enforce both pre- and post-nuptial agreements, as long as the agreements are not unreasonable and do not attempt to hide material information (such as the amount or types of assets each spouse possesses that will be covered by the agreement). Therefore, the court's main role with respect to pre- and post-nuptial agreements is to ensure that they are reasonable and will not leave one spouse without recourse or a means to support him/herself. Of course, the court will also ensure that children are protected even if pre- or post-nuptial agreements purport to award custody to or require support from a parent. As with all custody decisions, even where a pre- or post-nuptial agreement exists, the court will always take into account the best interests of children.

24. On what bases may her parental rights be terminated without her consent?

Because she is the natural mother of Marianne and William, Abigail's parental rights can only be terminated without her consent if a court finds by clear and convincing evidence that she is an unfit parent. You should advise her, that, as a natural parent, she has a fundamental right to care for and raise her own children.

In advising Abigail, you should explain what bases a court would have for finding her to be an unfit parent. First, she may be found to be unfit if she habitually neglects her children. Given the young age of her children, this may include a failure to feed them, clothe them, or look after them in an adequate way. Second, if she abuses her children, they may be taken from her involuntarily. Third, if she abandons them, the state may take over their care and terminate her parental rights. Fourth, if she is irreversibly mentally unstable or insane, the court may terminate her rights to her children because she will be unfit to care for or raise them.

In order to terminate Abigail's rights, the state will have to give her fair notice of its intention to seek such a termination in court. She must have an opportunity to present her case, although, as it will not be a criminal proceeding, she will not necessarily have a right to an attorney, except where failure to provide her with one would render the proceedings unfair.

25. If Abigail's parental rights are validly terminated, who will have standing to adopt Marianne and William?

In order for Marianne and William to be adopted at all, their biological father's rights must also be terminated. This may be accomplished in either of two ways: either (1) the father may voluntarily terminate his rights, or consent to their termination, or (2) the court may terminate the father's rights under the same standards discussed in Answer #24.

Assuming that the rights of the father are not at issue in this question, however, if the court does choose to terminate Abigail's parental rights, first in line to adopt Marianne and William would be close biological relatives, such as aunts or uncles, cousins, or grand-parents. A court will almost always prefer to keep siblings together, when possible, and to keep children with biological relatives. Note that a court will use the best interests of the child test in making adoption decisions, and most courts will feel that it is in the best interests of a child to be adopted by biological family members.

Absent any biological relatives who are willing or able to care for them, next in line to adopt William and Marianne would be any foster parents who have cared for them during the period of time that Abigail's termination proceeding was pending. If foster parents are found to be fit, it will probably be in the best interests of the children to keep them in a familiar environment.

If no relatives or foster parents are found, other fit persons may petition to adopt them. Note that, in many states, people of other races or religions will probably be eligible to adopt William and Marianne, as will people who are homosexual. Because of William and Marianne's young ages, they probably will not have to consent to the adoption. However, the court may take their feelings into consideration in making its final adoption determination.

COMMUNITY PROPERTY

I. INTRODUCTION

This section will give you a close look at one state's laws governing the distribution of assets and liabilities acquired and incurred before, during, and after a divorce has been filed. This section focuses on California's laws governing property distribution. California terms its property distribution regime "community property," and their laws dictate that assets acquired during the marriage are under the joint control of both spouses, and all assets are equally divided upon divorce. This differs from most states, which apply a "title theory" of property during the marriage. However, this distinction only applies to how couples handle their property during a marriage. During a marriage, title theory states permit whichever spouse holds title to a property to manage and dispose of it at his or her discretion. Community property states like California provide each spouse with equal rights concerning how property is treated during the marriage. However, upon dissolution, most states follow the regime of equitable distribution, which presumes an equal distribution, but permits courts to take into consideration any "equitable" factors that may justify an unequal distribution. A few states do not give any consideration to those factors and automatically provide for an equal distribution of the marital estate. Many of the concepts explored here are applicable to how all states handle marital and non-marital property distribution upon divorce. The heart of the community property or equitable distribution system involves classifying all property held by a married person as either community or marital property, or separate or non-marital property. Classification is of vital importance because once the property is classified, other consequences such as management and control, the rights of creditors and the division of the property on death or dissolution follow necessarily.

A. Property Defined

(non-marital)

1. **Property** is defined in Civil Code § 5110. The statutory definition basically includes any property acquired by a married California domiciliary that does not fall within one of the categories of separate property. The statute states that community property includes all real property situated in California and all personal property wherever situated acquired during marriage by a married person while domiciled in this state. Case law has expanded this definition to encompass even out-of-state real property by use of the tracing principle, discussed below.

B. Basic Principles

In addition to these two basic definitions, there are three basic principles that run throughout the California community property system.

1. The Equality Principle

The equality principle means that the spouses have present, existing, and equal interests in community property. Their relative contributions to the community property cannot be put at issue; they are conclusively presumed to be equal. Each spouse owns an individual one-half interest in all of the community property regardless of which spouse actually acquired a particular asset. (Civil Code § 5105)

2. The Tracing Principle

The second principle is the tracing principle. Changes in form do not change the underlying classification of the property as community or separate property. We trace an asset back to the original source of funds or property that was used to acquire it, and classify it accordingly.

Example:

Suppose that H inherited $25,000 during marriage. He initially put that $25,000 in a savings account. Later he transferred it to a checking account, withdrew the money and bought stock, and then sold the stock and used the proceeds to buy a car. The classification of the car is at issue. We trace the car back to the stock, back to the bank accounts, back to the inheritance. Because property inherited by a spouse is separate property, the car must be classified as separate property.

A corollary of the tracing principle is that community property, when used or invested, produces community property, and that separate property, when used or invested, produces separate property. Therefore the tracing principle encompasses not only changes in form, such as proceeds from the sale or exchange of an asset, but also rents, profits, dividends, or other forms of income derived from the asset.

Example:

Suppose that W inherited 100 shares of ABC stock from her father. Every year the stock produced dividends. Those dividends take on the classification of the underlying stock, here, separate property. If the stock increased in value the increase in value would likewise be separate property. Suppose that instead of inheriting the stock, W had purchased it with her earnings during marriage. Any dividends would again take on the underlying classification of the stock, in this case, community property. If the stock increased in value, the increase would also be community property.

3. The Contractual Modification Principle

Under the principle of contractual modification, the operation of the community property system may be significantly modified or limited by agreement between the spouses. Such agreement may take place prior to marriage ("prenuptial," "antenuptial," or "premarital") or during the marriage.

Under the principle of contractual modification, the spouses themselves can determine how their property will be classified. They can agree that what would generally be classified as community property will be the separate property of one

FAMILY LAW

or the other. Conversely, they can change or transmute separate property to community property by agreement. In effect, the spouses can contract themselves out of the community property system.

II. THE CLASSIFICATION PROCESS

A. The General Presumption of Community Property

There is a rebuttable presumption that all property acquired by a married person is community property. Therefore, the first stage of the classification process requires an inquiry as to the time of acquisition: Was the asset at issue acquired before marriage or during marriage? If it was acquired before marriage, then it falls within one of the statutory definitions of separate property and will be classified accordingly. But if it was acquired during marriage, it comes within this general presumption of community property.

California courts have long declared that there is a general presumption that property acquired during the marriage is community property. The general presumption comes into play once it is proven that the property in question was acquired during the marriage. In most cases, there will be evidence as to the time of acquisition. In cases where there is little or no evidence as to the manner or time of acquisition, the courts have held that possession during marriage, coupled with other factors, may give rise to the general presumption. These other factors may include a lengthy marriage or the absence of separate property that could have been used for the acquisition.

B. Rebuttal of the General Presumption

The general presumption is a rebuttable presumption. There are three primary methods of rebutting or avoiding the general presumption:

1) Tracing the disputed asset back to a separate property source;

2) Showing facts giving rise to one of the special presumptions; or

3) Showing an agreement between the spouses.

1. Tracing to Separate Property Sources

The usual method of rebutting the general presumption is to trace the asset at issue back to a separate property source.

a. Nature of acquisition: gift or inheritance

One major category of separate property is based on the *nature* of the acquisition. If property is received as a gift or inheritance, it is the separate property of the acquiring spouse, even if the asset was acquired during marriage. So if the asset at issue can be *traced* to a gift or inheritance received by one spouse, even though acquired during marriage, the asset can be classified as separate property. The burden of tracing the property back to a separate property source will be on the spouse seeking to establish the separate property classification.

b. **Time of acquisition**

Another major category of separate property is determined by the *time* of the acquisition. Property acquired prior to marriage is the separate property of the acquiring spouse. Similarly, property acquired by a spouse after separation is separate property.

(1) **Premarriage acquisitions**

If one spouse can trace the asset at issue back to property owned prior to marriage, the spouse can rebut the general presumption and the asset will be classified as separate property

Note that the asset must be traced back to a property right that existed before marriage. Normally this is not an issue but such a problem can arise.

Example:

Suppose H entered onto Blackacre and began adverse possession two years prior to marriage. Three years after marriage, the statute of limitations runs and husband acquires title to Blackacre. At dissolution, he claims that Blackacre is his separate property by tracing it back to his entry premarriage. Resolution of this problem might depend on whether the court views husband as having a "property right" before marriage. If Blackacre had been purchased by the husband prior to marriage but he did not receive a valid deed, the court might find that he had an equitable right that arose before marriage.

Compare:

Suppose that H had entered onto Blackacre before marriage as a trespasser. After marriage, he exploited the nuisance value of his actions and gave up possession of half of the tract in exchange for a deed from the rightful owner to the balance of the tract. Here, the court could hold that H had not acquired any property rights prior to marriage, that he was merely a trespasser, and therefore the property was acquired during marriage and should be classified as community property. See *Pancoast v. Pancoast*, 57 Cal. 320 (1881).

Exception:

Some federal land grant and homestead statutes have been interpreted as requiring title to land acquired pursuant to this legislation to be awarded to the spouse who (1) initially went into possession of the land, or (2) was living on the land when title vested. This is really a question of federal preemption.

To summarize, it is possible to rebut the general presumption by tracing, if it can be shown that there was an actual property right owned before marriage.

(2) Post-separation acquisitions

If the spouse can show that the asset at issue was acquired with post-separation earnings, the asset may be classified as separate property. Under Civil Code § 5118, the earnings and accumulations of the spouses while living separate and apart are the separate property of the acquiring spouse. This rule once applied only to the earnings of the wife, but legislation enacted in 1972 make it equally applicable to both spouses, and the 1972 amendment has been held retroactive. With regard to this category of separate property, the cases frequently turn on the ***definition of separation.*** Spouses are deemed to be living "separate and apart" when at least one of them views their separation as permanent and either (i) communicates this belief to the other, or (ii) the circumstances are such that the other spouse should have recognized that the former viewed their relationship as being permanently terminated. The basic rule applied by the courts is that the parties' conduct must evidence a complete and final break in the marital relationship. The question is whether the spouses have come to a parting of the ways with no present intent of resuming marital relations.

Physical separation is not determinative. Therefore, the mere fact that the spouses reside in different locations due to job or health reasons does not establish that they are living separate and apart under Civil Code § 5118. The key factor is an intent not to continue the marital relationship. The fact that the wife moved out of the family home and filed a dissolution petition was held not to establish as a matter of law that the parties were living separate and apart within the meaning of § 5118. *Marriage of Marsden*, 130 CA3d 426, 181 CR 910 (1982). In the *Marsden* case, the wife testified that although she filed a dissolution petition, she did not want divorce, instead, she wanted to work out the couple's difficulties. Evidence also showed that parties continued their sexual relationship, saw a marriage counselor, and traveled together.

Furthermore, the intent not to resume the marriage relationship must be manifested by conduct. In *Marriage of Baragry*, 73 Cal. Ct. App.3d 444 (1977), the husband moved out of the house and lived with his girlfriend. The court said these factors did not establish that the husband and wife were living separate and apart where the spouses preserved the facade of their marriage, and the husband brought home his laundry every week.

(3) Death post-dissolution

If a person dies more than four years after the marriage was terminated by dissolution, the general presumption that property acquired during marriage is community property does not apply to the decedent's estate. Civil Code § 5111.

C. The Special Presumptions

The special presumptions are generally based on the form of title. They may be grouped into two broad categories: (1) acquisitions by a married woman in her name alone and (2) co-ownership presumptions.

1. Pre-1975 Acquisitions by a Married Woman

Civil Code § 5110 raises a special presumption of separate property where a title in writing was acquired by a married woman prior to January 1, 1975. This special presumption does not apply to acquisitions after that date.

The rationale for the special presumption involves the fact that prior to 1975, the husband had the sole right to manage and control the community property with the limited exception of the wife's earnings. If a married man executed a conveyance to his wife, or if he permitted title to be taken in his wife's name alone, he must have intended to change the property rights of himself and his wife. He was not indulging in an idle act. The courts presume that the husband intended a gift to his wife. The husband can rebut the presumption, but it is not sufficient to merely trace the property to a separate property source.

Example:

In 1970 H used $100,000 of community property earnings to acquire a piece of real property. Title was taken in W's name alone. H and W are now getting divorced in 1989 and H wants to establish that the realty is community property. The facts here — i.e., the form of title — give rise to the special presumption. To rebut it, H will have to do more than trace that property back to the community property earnings. He must show that he had no intent to make a gift and that there was another reason for the form of title chosen.

Note that after 1951, a married woman had management and control rights over her own earnings. The question then is whether the special presumption should apply where the wife used her own earnings to acquire an asset and took title in her name alone. The California Supreme Court has held that the special presumption should not apply where the wife had management and control over the funds in question, because there is no basis for presuming a gift by the husband.

Thus the general presumption of community property should apply. *Marriage of Mix*, 145 Cal.3d 604 (1975).

Example:

Suppose that in 1970, W used her own earnings to buy 100 shares of ABC stock, taking title to the stock in her name alone. Since she had management and control over the funds used to acquire the stock, we cannot say that her husband intended to make a gift to her. So the stock should simply be within the general presumption of community property.

2. **Co-ownership Presumptions**

a. **Acquisitions by a married woman and another person**

The presumption that property interests acquired prior to 1975 by a married woman by written instrument are her separate property applies also to undivided interests held by a married woman with another person: the wife is deemed to hold her interest as a tenant in common; her share is her separate property. This rule was applied even where the husband and wife took title as tenants in common. The wife's interest was presumptively her separate property, while the husband's interest was presumptively community property. The result was that the wife had a three-fourths interest in the property and the husband only a one-fourth interest.

To counteract this strange result, the legislature added another special presumption: where property is acquired by husband and wife in an instrument in which they are described as husband and wife, the property is presumptively community property. So if the title instrument reads:

John Jones & Mary Jones, husband and wife

the property is presumptively community property. This is a special community property presumption and rebuttal of this special presumption is very difficult. It cannot be rebutted by mere tracing. It can only be rebutted by evidence of a written agreement or understanding between the spouses. (See discussion of Civil Code § 4800.1 below.)

b. **Joint Tenancy**

Despite the fact that California is a community property jurisdiction, many married couples in California hold most of their property in joint tenancy. Frequently married persons use community funds to purchase an asset, and then take title to the asset in joint tenancy form; e.g., "John Jones and Mary Jones, husband and wife, as joint tenants with right of survivorship." A problem may arise because the legal incidents of joint tenancy are different in several respects from community property. One of the most significant differences is that each spouse is free to will away his or her half of the community property, but joint tenancy property passes to the surviving joint tenant by operation of law.

(1) The judicial presumption

Because the legal incidents of the two forms of ownership are different, California courts repeatedly have held that a community property estate and a joint tenancy cannot coexist in the same item of property. The asset must be one or the other, it cannot be both. Over the years, the California courts developed a judicial presumption regarding the use of community property funds to purchase an asset where title is taken in joint tenancy. The courts indicated that the act of taking title in joint tenancy in effect gives rise to a rebuttable presumption that a joint tenancy was intended, but such presumption can be rebutted by evidence of an understanding or mutual intent to the contrary. Litigation involving the question of joint tenancy vs. community property has been extensive, but the cases offer little guidance in determining what type of evidence is sufficient to overcome the judicial joint tenancy presumption. However, it is clear that the secret intent of one spouse, undisclosed to the other, that the property be community is not sufficient. But the mutual ignorance of both spouses as to the meaning and effect of joint tenancy may be sufficient to rebut the judicial joint tenancy presumption.

(2) Statutory presumptions

In 1983 the Legislature enacted Civil Code § 4800.1, which creates a special community property presumption applicable to assets held in joint tenancy. Civil Code § 4800.2 was enacted at the same time.

Civil Code § 4800.1

For purposes of dissolution, any property acquired by husband and wife in joint form is presumed to be community property. The community presumption can be rebutted only by:

1) a clear statement in the title instrument that the property is separate property and not community property, or

2) a written agreement between the spouses that the property is separate property.

The community property presumption cannot be rebutted by evidence that the disputed asset was a gift and the donor intended to create a joint tenancy. Nor can it be rebutted by showing that one spouse furnished the entire consideration for the asset and had no donative intent. It can be rebutted only by written evidence.

Civil Code § 4800.2

Civil Code § 4800.2 applies to a division of community property in a dissolution proceeding. When property is determined to be community property but one spouse can establish that he or she contributed separate property to the community property acquisition or to an improvement of community property, the spouse will be entitled to reimbursement in the absence of a written waiver.

By their terms, Civil Code §§ 4800.1 and 4800.2 apply to any case filed after January 1, 1984; however, case law indicates that these statutes cannot be constitutionally applied to property acquired prior to January 1, 1984.

Example of operation of §§ 4800.1 and 4800.2:

Suppose that H and W decided to buy a piece of commercial realty which had a purchase price of $100,000. W had inherited $100,000 from her father, and this separate property was used to buy the property. Title was taken in the names of H and W as joint tenants with right of survivorship. Twenty years later the couple gets divorced. The property is now worth $500,000.

Under § 4800.1 the property is presumed to be community property. W argues: "I can trace the entire purchase price to my separate property. Therefore I should get the current value of the property as my separate property." This argument would not succeed under prior case law and will not succeed under the current statutes. Under Civil Code § 4800.1, W can rebut the community property presumption only by showing a written agreement that the property was to be retained as her separate property. However, by virtue of § 4800.2, she will probably be entitled to reimbursement for her separate property contribution, i.e., the original $100,000 purchase price. She would not be entitled to interest or appreciation.

Note that these statutes apply only on dissolution. In a death situation, the judicially created presumption regarding joint tenancy would still apply. Note also that Civil Code § 4800.1 was amended in 1986 to include not only joint tenancy property, but other concurrent forms of ownership, including tenancy in common, tenancy by the entirety and community property.

D. Classification by Interspousal Agreement

It may be possible to overcome the general presumption of community property by agreement between the spouses that the property be separate property. As was noted at page 3 of the Outline, a major tenet of the California community property system is the fact that operation of the system may be modified or limited by an agreement between the spouses. These agreements are frequently referred to as "transmutation agreements."

The contractual modification principle is recognized in Civil Code § 5103, which provides that a husband and wife may enter into any transaction with each other respecting property which either might, if unmarried. In addition, Civil Code § 5110.710 expressly provides for the transmutation of community property to separate property and vice-versa.

Under the principle of contractual modification, the spouses themselves can determine how their property will be classified. They can agree that what would ordinarily be classified as community will be the separate property of one or the other. Conversely, they can transmute separate property to community property by agreement. In effect, the spouses can contract themselves out of the community property system. For example, suppose that upon getting married, the spouses agree that the earnings and accumulations of each will be the acquiring spouse's separate property. This type of agreement would result in little, if any, community property.

Interspousal contracts can take a variety of forms. They can relate to all of the couple's property or to only one or two specific assets. They can cover property in existence or property to be acquired in the future. Thus a married couple can change or transmute separate to community property by agreement and can also transmute community to separate property by agreement. The California courts have been very liberal about recognizing and enforcing interspousal agreements executed prior to January 1, 1985. Post-1985 agreements must now meet certain statutory formal requirements.

1. **Pre-1985 Agreements**

   Interspousal agreements made prior to January 1, 1985, may be exceedingly informal and yet still legally enforceable.

   1) The courts have held repeatedly that consideration is not necessary to support a transmutation agreement; all that is required is the mutual asset of the spouses.

   2) The courts have held that such agreements are fully executed at the time they are made. This means that even oral agreements respecting real property can be enforced, since fully executed agreements are outside the Statute of Frauds.

   A similar approach has also been applied to oral premarital agreements which were required by Civil Code § 5134 to be written. That is, the court may treat such an agreement as fully executed, either by the fact of marriage or subsequent ratification.

However, there seems to be one major exception to the courts' willingness to recognize and enforce oral agreements: where an interspousal agreement purports to create survivorship rights, the courts are much more reluctant to forgo the requirement of a writing. For example, where couples have attempted to orally transmute community property into joint tenancy property, the courts have held that a writing is required. Civil Code § 683 requires a writing for the creation of a joint tenancy.

2. **Post-1985 Interspousal Transmutation Agreements**

With regard to transmutation agreements made after January 1, 1985, the legislature has imposed the following requirements (Civil Code § 5110.730):

a. A transmutation of either real or personal property must be made in writing and "joined in, consented to, or accepted by the spouse whose interest in the property is affected." The writing requirement does not apply to interspousal gifts of clothing, jewelry, or other tangible personal items used primarily by the donee spouse so long as the gift is "not substantial in value taking into account the circumstances of the marriage."

    Example:

    For their five-year anniversary, Husband presents Wife with an expensive diamond ring. Shortly thereafter wife files a petition for divorce. The trial court declared the ring to be wife's separate property noting "[the husband] purchased a diamond of substantial value using community funds and unilaterally gave it [to the wife] at or about the time of their fifth wedding anniversary as a gift, with a card announcing his congratulations." Husband appealed and the court reversed holding, **"In light of the clear language of the statute it would be inappropriate to hold the transmutation of jewelry that was substantial in value taking into account the circumstances of the marriages without the required writing."** *In re marriage of Steinburger*, (2001) California Court of Appeal, 6th District Docket #H020669.

b. A transmutation of real property is not effective as to third parties without notice unless it has been recorded. Note also that a transmutation is subject to the laws governing fraudulent transfers.

3. **Post-1986 Premarital Agreements**

With respect to premarital agreements executed after January 1, 1986, California has adopted the Uniform Premarital Agreement Act. The Uniform Act provides that a premarital agreement must be in writing and signed by both parties. It is enforceable without consideration and becomes effective on marriage. (Civil Code §§ 5311, 5313)

III. SPECIAL CLASSIFICATION PROBLEMS

The following sections deal with application of the basic classification rules to some special problems. These problems arise largely because many married people do not keep their separate property and community property wholly segregated. They may mix funds in a bank account/or acquire an asset using a combination of funds. They may expend community assets in operating a separate property business. They may use separate property to improve community property, or vice versa. These kinds of situations can give rise to serious classification problems when the asset must be classed for purposes of division on dissolution, division on death, or attachment by creditors.

A. Commingled Funds

"Commingling" refers to the combining or intermixing of community and separate funds in a common mass or pool. The most common example involves the deposit of both community property and separate property funds in a single bank account during marriage. If deposits are made at one time, no withdrawals are made and records are kept as to the nature of the deposits, then classification would be relatively easy.

The account can be viewed as an acquisition during marriage and within the general presumption of community property. However, the spouse seeking to establish the separate character of a portion of the account can rebut the general presumption by directly tracing that portion of the funds to a separate property source.

Example:

W inherited $50,000 from her father. She put the $50,000 together with $100,000 in community savings into one bank account. No further actions were taken with respect to the account. At dissolution the account is put at issue. The account was acquired during marriage and is therefore within general presumption. But W may be able to rebut the general presumption if she can trace $50,000 or $\frac{1}{3}$ of the $150,000 funds to a separate property source, her inheritance. If she has no rebuttal evidence or insufficient rebuttal evidence then the entire account will be classified as community property by virtue of the general presumption.

Where there are deposits and withdrawals over a period of time, and the commingled funds are used to purchase other assets, the classification problems become more complicated. The controlling principles remain the same, however. The asset is within the general presumption, but rebuttal may be accomplished by tracing. Two different types of tracing may be used, depending on the facts of the case and the type of evidence available.

1. Direct Tracing

If sufficient records have been kept as to the nature of deposits and withdrawals, rebuttal may be achieved by direct tracing.

Example:

W put separate property inheritance of $50,000 into a bank account which contains $100,000 of community property funds. Thereafter W withdrew $50,000 and purchased stock. At dissolution proceedings, classification of the stock is at issue. The stock is within the general presumption but if W has kept records showing that she deposited and withdrew $50,000 of her separate property to buy the stock, then the stock may be classified as her separate property.

2. **Indirect Tracing (Family Expense Presumption)**

If direct evidence is lacking, as it may well be if the spouses have not kept accurate records of the nature of every deposit and withdrawal, a more indirect type of tracing may be used. This method of indirect tracing is based on the judicial presumption that family expenses are paid from community funds (commonly known as the family expense presumption).

If it can be established that at the time the disputed asset was acquired, the community funds in the account had been exhausted by family expenses, then the balance in the account must necessarily have been separate property. Any item purchased at that point must have been acquired with separate property and would therefore be classified as separate property.

Example:

Suppose that $100,000 of community property and $50,000 of W's separate property were deposited into a single account. Some years later, W withdrew $50,000 to buy stock. If W can show that at the time of the withdrawal, the community expenses had used up $100,000, then the balance in the account must have been her separate property.

Note that the spouse must establish that the community expenses were in excess of the community funds at the time the stock was acquired. The time of acquisition is controlling; total recapitulation at the end of the marriage is not sufficient.

Example:

Again, suppose the bank account contained $100,000 community property earnings and $50,000 of W's separate property. At some point during the couple's five-year marriage, W bought stock costing $50,000. W can show that over the five-year period, the community expenses exceeded $100,000 and argues that the stock must therefore have been purchased with separate property. The California courts have held that this type of evidence is not sufficient. W would have to show that at the time she acquired the stock, community property funds had been exhausted by family expenses.

Now suppose that W cannot show exhaustion of community property funds at the time of acquisition, but claims that if the court refuses to classify the stock as her separate property, that means that her separate property was used for family expenses, and she should at least get reimbursement. This argument has been made and rejected by the California courts. In this situation, the courts have indicated that a gift of separate property funds to the community will be presumed.

One exception to the non-reimbursement rule arises in the living separate and apart context. If a spouse pays family living expenses while living separate and apart from the other spouse, reimbursement will be appropriate, unless the payments were made to fulfill support obligations or there was an agreement that the payments would not be reimbursed.

3. De Minimus Rule

If it is impossible to trace either directly or indirectly the separate and community contributions to the commingled funds or assets purchased with commingled funds, the general presumption of community property controls. However, if the respective amounts of community and separate contributions can be established, but if the amount of the community property contribution is insignificant, the court may disregard it. This is known as the *de minimus* rule.

B. Business Profits

Suppose that the husband owned and operated a business prior to marriage. At the time that the husband and wife were married, the business was worth $100,000. The husband continued to work in the business during marriage. Some years later the parties get divorced, and the business is now worth $500,000. So there has been a $400,000 increase in the value of the business during marriage.

The general tracing rule normally mandates that profits and gains derived from separate property are classified as separate property. But here the husband has been contributing a community asset, i.e., his time, energy, and skill to the business. Where both separate property and community property combine in the production of new wealth California courts have determined that the new production should be apportioned according to the relative separate and community contributions. This means that the $400,000 gain must be apportioned on the basis of husband's community property efforts during marriage and the original separate property capital investment. The method of apportionment depends in part upon the type of evidence available.

1. Complete Evidence Approach

If there is clear evidence of both the normal rate of return on the separate property capital and the value of the community services, no special apportionment formula is necessary. The gain or profits can simply be apportioned on the basis of the relative established contributions.

Example:

Suppose that the marriage in question lasted 20 years. It is shown that husband worked in the business throughout this period. There is evidence that a fair return on capital for the type of business and time in question would be 10% per year. There is also expert testimony that the value of husband's managements skills was $10,000 per year.

This is complete evidence of the relative contributions of both factors:

$100,000 invested at 10% per year over 20 years would produce $200,000 (without compounding), $10,000 per year for 20 years would also produce $200,000.

In the above example, we would simply apportion the $400,000 gain on the basis of the established contributions: 50% separate property and 50% community property. Of course, the original $100,000 is the husband's separate property. Therefore we have accounted for the entire present fair market value of the business.

2. **Incomplete Evidence Approaches**

In many cases, clear evidence of the relative contributions of both factors does not exist. The evidence of the value of the spouse's services or of the normal rate of return on the particular kind of capital may be incomplete or inconclusive. California courts have developed two different approaches to deal with these types of situations.

a. **The *Pereira* approach**

One method, frequently called the *Pereira* approach, involves the allocation of a fair return on the spouse's separate property investment as separate income, and then the allocation of any excess to the community. If there is no evidence of what a fair rate of return would be, the court may use the legal interest rate, which is currently 10%.

If this method is applied to the example above, the court could find that $200,000 of the gain represents separate property income ($100,000 x 10% x 20 years). The balance ($200,000) would be allocated to the community.

If the husband could prove that capital in this type of business was generally highly productive, e.g., produced a return of 15% per annum, then the court could use the 15% rate. This would result in an allocation of $300,000 to separate property and only $100,000 to community property (15% x $100,000 x 20 years).

b. The *Van Camp* approach

The alternative approach, commonly called the *Van Camp* approach, takes the opposite tack. Under the *Van Camp* approach, the court determines the reasonable value of the spouse's services, allocates that amount to the community, and treats the balance as separate property.

Suppose that in the example above there was no evidence of the productivity rate of capital, but that there was expert testimony that the value of the husband's management skills was $15,000 per year. Under *Van Camp* the court would multiply this by the number of years husband worked in the business during marriage (20 years), and allocate that amount ($300,000) to the community, and the balance ($100,000) would be separate property.

Suppose that in addition to the evidence of the value of his management services the husband can show that $10,000 worth of profits were withdrawn from the business each year and were used to pay the family's living expenses. This means that in addition to the $400,000 gain, the business was producing an additional $10,000 in profits each year, or $200,000 over the marriage, which was paid out to the community. Therefore, the community has already received some compensation for the community efforts. The expert testimony shows that it is entitled to $300,000 and it has already received $200,000. So the community is only entitled to an additional $100,000. The balance of the gain ($300,000) would be allocated to the husband's separate estate.

3. Other Applications of Business Profits Apportionment Principles

The apportionment of profits doctrine was first developed in cases involving a separate property business, but has since been applied in other contexts; for example, farming operations and real estate and securities investments. The apportionment doctrine can be applied wherever there is some significant community labor contribution to the increase of separate property capital.

The apportionment of business profits doctrine also has application where one spouse continues to manage a community property business while living separate and apart from the other spouse. For example, suppose that the spouses own a community property business operated by one spouse. The spouses separate, and are living separate and apart within the meaning of Civil Code § 5118. The managing spouse continues to operate the business. After separation, a spouse's time, energy, and skill are the separate property of the spouse. Suppose that the business produces profits and increases in value during separation. Again there are two assets — the community property capital and the separate property time, energy, and skill contributing to the production of new wealth. The apportionment rules, either *Pereira* or *Van Camp* depending on the evidence, can be applied to this situation. This situation is sometimes said to involve "reverse apportionment."

4. Selection of *Pereira* or *Van Camp* Approaches

In any given case, a question may arise as to which approach is more appropriate: *Pereira* or *Van Camp*. The answer depends partly on the kind of evidence available: if there is evidence of the reasonable value of the spouse's services, then *Van Camp* could be applied. If there is no such evidence, then *Pereira* can be applied, using either the legal rate of return or whatever rate is shown by the facts to be appropriate. Note that trial courts have been given wide discretion in choosing which approach to use. The trial judge should select whatever approach will achieve substantial justice between the parties, i.e., an equitable result.

C. Installment Acquisitions

Married couples frequently use both separate and community property in the acquisition of major assets, particularly those acquired over time. In certain kinds of transactions, ownership interests in an asset are acquired on a piecemeal basis over time. Common examples include pensions, life insurance, and real property acquired under an installment sales contract. The initial transaction in the acquisition of such an asset may have occurred prior to marriage, with the acquisition completed during marriage. Even where the entire acquisition took place during marriage, separate property may have been used for the initial payments, with later payments coming from community funds.

In classifying such acquisitions, some of the early California cases followed the parent Spanish-Mexican system and used an inception of right theory. Under this theory, the asset was classified as of the inception of the right; that is when the initial interest in the property was acquired. If funds of a different classification were used to complete the acquisition, reimbursement was a possibility, but there was no apportionment of the property itself.

However, later California cases developed a different approach, reasoning that when an asset is acquired over time by installment payments, the asset should be apportioned on the basis of community and separate contributions to the purchase price and apportioned accordingly. The apportionment theory has been used in cases involving installment land contracts and life insurance proceeds.

1. Installment Land Sale Contracts

Suppose that prior to marriage the husband decided to purchase Blackacre for $100,000. The seller agreed to sell Blackacre to the husband on an installment basis. The husband put $20,000 down, and agreed to pay the balance of the purchase price in installments of $10,000 per year over the next eight years. After making one installment payment, the husband married his wife. He continued to make the annual installment payments out of his earnings. After ten years of marriage, the husband and wife get divorced.

Blackacre is worth $150,000 at the time of dissolution. How should the court classify Blackacre? Look to the source of the payments on the purchase price. Here, the down payment of $20,000 and one installment payment of $10,000 were paid prior to marriage, and thus from the husband's separate property. Seven installment payments ($70,000) came from earnings during marriage, thus from community property. An apportionment can be made on the basis of these relative contributions to the total payments.

$$30,000/100,000 = 3/10 \text{ separate property}$$
$$70,000/100,000 = 7/10 \text{ community property}$$

These ratios can then be applied to the equity value of Blackacre at the time of dissolution: $45,000 would be husband's separate property; $105,000 would be community property (to be divided equally between husband and wife).

2. Life insurance proceeds

Where premiums on a life insurance policy were paid partly from community property funds and partly from separate funds, and the insured spouse dies, the insurance proceeds will be subject to apportionment. The courts have apportioned the proceeds on the basis of the nature of the premium payments.

Example:

Suppose that prior to marriage H took out a policy of life insurance on his own life, designating his mother as the beneficiary of the $90,000 proceeds payable in event of H's death. H paid the quarterly premium payments out of his earnings. Some years later, H married W, and continued to pay the premium payments out of his earnings. After 20 years of marriage, H dies. Now the question is who is entitled to the insurance proceeds. To the extent that the proceeds represent community property, the surviving spouse would be entitled to one-half of the community portion.

In this example, if one-third of the total premium payments was paid prior to marriage, and two-thirds were paid from community earnings during marriage, then one-third of the proceeds would be separate property ($30,000) and two-thirds would be community property ($60,000). Therefore, W would be entitled to one-half of the community's interest, or $30,000. The balance would go to the designated beneficiary, the husband's mother.

3. Failure to disclose community property assets

Where a spouse actively conceals from the other spouse community property assets to avoid forfeiture or division that spouse is committing fraud with the meaning of Civil Code section 3294. Fraud under Civil Code 3294 provides in pertinent part: **"(a) In an action for the breach of an obligation not arising**

from contract, where it is proven by clear and convincing evidence that the defendant has been guilty of oppression, fraud or malice, the plaintiff, in addition to the actual damages, may recover damages for the sake of example and by way of punishing the defendant."

Example:

A spouse who won a share of the California State Lottery jackpot and actively concealed the jackpot during her divorce and settlement agreements was found guilty of fraud. As a result, the court awarded the entire amount of the Lottery jackpot to the other spouse. *In re Marriage of Denise and Thomas Rossi*, California Court of Appeals, Second Appellate District, docket #B141041 (2001).

4. **Community property settlements are subject to creditor's claims**

Divorce decrees and community property asset divisions may be subject to creditor claims under the Uniform Fraudulent Transfer Act. To attach assets, the court must find that a spouse made a fraudulent transfer of a valuable asset during divorce proceedings to avoid attachment by a creditor.

Example:

Plaintiff filed an action against defendant, a married man, for paternity of her child. After the court awards the plaintiff a decree of child support, defendant's wife files for divorce. In the divorce decree, defendant keeps the medical practice while surrendering the family residence to the ex-wife. Defendant then quits his medical practice and moves in with his mother and stops making child support payments to the plaintiff. Plaintiff sues defendant and his ex-wife claiming the transfer of the house was a clear attempt to circumvent the earlier child support decree. Held: Marital property settlement agreements and judgments of dissolution are subject to creditor's claims under the Uniform Fraudulent transfer act. *Mejia v. Reed*, 2002 DJDAR 3455 the Court of Appeals for the Sixth Appellate District.

D. **Borrowed Funds and Credit Acquisitions**

Property acquired during marriage through a credit or loan transaction comes within the general presumption of community property but the general presumption can be rebutted by use of the tracing principles, showing that separate property produced the acquisition. In cases involving borrowed funds or credit acquisitions the type of tracing evidence may be quite different from other types of cases.

Example:

Suppose that during marriage H went to a lending institution such as a bank or a savings and loan and borrowed $5,000. He later used the $5,000 to purchase stock. Assume that the classification of the stock is now at issue in dissolution proceedings. The stock is clearly within the general presumption of community property, but H wants to establish that the stock is his separate property. H can easily trace the stock back to the loan proceeds. But where did the loan proceeds come from — the bank? The question, then is, what induced the bank to make the loan? Realistically, the bank was probably relying on a variety of factors such as the husband's credit record, the husband's earning capacity, and the husband's net worth. But California courts have traditionally classified loan proceeds on the basis of the primary intent of the lender. If H can show that the bank was relying on some separate asset when it made the loan, then the court may classify the loan proceeds as H's separate property.

Recent case law requires that the separate property proponent establish that the lender was relying solely on separate property when it made the loan. *In re Marriage of Grinius,* 166 Cal. Ct. App. 1179, (1985).

Example:

Suppose that H owned Blackacre as his separate property and put up Blackacre as collateral for the loan. He may be able to show that the loan was produced by this separate property, i.e., that the lender was relying solely on the security interest in Blackacre when it made the loan. If he can prove this, then the stock would be classified as his separate property.

Suppose in the above example that the loan proceeds are determined to be the husband's separate property and the stock is classified accordingly as the husband's separate property. Suppose that it is also shown that husband repaid the loan using his earnings during marriage. Using the credit acquisition approach, the community may be entitled to reimbursement, but it would not have any ownership interest in the stock itself.

The basic rule for classifying borrowed funds and credit acquisitions is to look to the intent of the lender. If the lender was relying solely on separate property to make the loan, the loan proceeds may be classified as separate property. Any asset purchased with those loan proceeds would likewise be classified as separate property. The preceding examples involved a loan taken out during marriage but produced by separate property of the husband. A similar result would be obtained if one spouse borrowed money prior to marriage.

Example:

Suppose that prior to marriage, H borrowed $1,000 from the bank and used the money to buy stock. Then H married W. The couple later gets divorced, and classification of the stock is at issue. Here the loan was taken out prior to marriage. The loan proceeds would necessarily be classified as separate property regardless of what induced the bank to make the loan. If H used community funds to pay off the loan, the community may be entitled to reimbursement, but H would own the stock as his separate property.

E. Purchase Money Secured Loan Transaction

The purchase money secured loan transaction represents a variation on the borrowed funds case. In this situation, the stock purchase and the loan transaction are closely interrelated. On occasion, California courts have treated this situation as being more akin to an installment transaction than a credit acquisition. In effect, the courts view the payments on the loan as if they were payments on the purchase price of the stock. So that if all of the payments came from community earnings, the stock would be classified as community property.

Example:

Suppose that prior to marriage W wanted to buy stock that costs $10,000. W did not have $10,000, so she went to the bank to borrow it. The bank said that it was willing to make the loan provided that the wife put up some security. W offered to put up the stock that she was purchasing as collateral. The bank agrees and makes the loan. W bought the stock and used the stock to secure the loan. Note that the loan here was secured by the asset being purchased with the loan proceeds. Then W marries H and paid off the loan using community funds. When H and W get divorced, the classification of the stock is at issue. Because this was a purchase money loan, the court might treat the community property payments on the loan as if they were payments for the purchase price of the stock, and classify the stock as entirely community property.

In the preceding example, it was assumed that the loan was totally repaid during marriage. But suppose that only a portion of the loan had been repaid and, at dissolution, there is still an outstanding loan balance. In this latter situation, the California courts have developed a sort of hybrid approach, combining both installment acquisition and credit acquisition theories. This approach, adopted by the California Supreme Court in the *Lucas* and *Moore* cases, has been applied in cases involving the acquisition of residential real property using a purchase money deed of trust. See *In re Marriage of Lucas*, 27 Cal.3d 808, (1980); *In re Marriage of Moore*, 28 Cal.3d 366, (1980).

Example:

Suppose that prior to marriage W decided to buy a house. The purchase price was $100,000. W had $20,000 to use as a down payment and borrowed $80,000 from a bank for the balance. The lender wanted security, so W agreed to execute a purchase money deed of trust as security. Thus the house that W purchased was being used as security for the loan. Shortly after this transaction, and before any loan payments are made, W married H. W used her earnings during marriage to make payments on the loan. Some years later H and W get divorced and classification of the house is at issue. Assume that the house is now worth $200,000, and that the loan balance is now $60,000.

In classifying the house, there are three elements that must be considered and classified:

(1) the down payment ($20,000) — W's separate property

(2) the loan proceeds ($80,000) — W's separate property

(3) principal payments made on the loan ($20,000) — community property.

The court will work out an apportionment on the basis of the contributions of these elements to the total purchase price:

Community Property: $\dfrac{20,000}{100,000} = \dfrac{1}{5}$

Separate Property: $\dfrac{20,000(\text{down}) + 80,000(\text{loan}) - 20,000(\text{CP})}{100,000} \quad \dfrac{4}{5}$

These ratios can then be applied to the current fair market value of the property:

$\dfrac{1}{5}$ x 200,000 = $40,000 community property

$\dfrac{4}{5}$ x 200,000 = $160,000 W's separate property

However, there is still an outstanding loan balance of $60,000. W's separate property estate was credited with the loan proceeds, and therefore it will be charged with the loan balance. Therefore as a practical matter, W gets $100,000 as her separate property.

F. Improvements

When real property is improved by one of the spouses, the improvement takes on the classification of the underlying real property. However, reimbursement may be in order, depending on the nature of the funds used in making the improvement, the nature of the estate improved and which spouse made the improvements.

1. Use of community funds to improve the other spouse's separate property

Suppose that W owns a house and a lot as her separate property, and that the husband uses $10,000 of community property funds to construct a swimming pool. The pool takes on the classification of the underlying realty — here, W's separate property. The question then is whether the community is entitled to reimbursement. Prior to 1975, when the husband had exclusive management and control of community property, the courts would have presumed a gift. This was a rebuttable presumption. The husband could rebut by showing a contrary agreement or understanding. Case law suggests that the gift presumption will continue to apply under the post-1975 management and control legislation.

2. **Use of community funds to improve the improver's separate property**

Suppose that H owns a house and lot as his separate property and suppose that he uses $10,000 of community property funds to construct a swimming pool. Again, the pool takes on the classification of the underlying realty but, here, reimbursement to the community would be appropriate. Otherwise, H would be enriching his own separate estate at the expense of the community. The next question is the measure of the reimbursement. California courts have held that the community is entitled to either the amount expended or the value added — whichever is greater. These rules have also been applied where one spouse uses community funds to pay taxes or assessments on his or her separate property.

3. **Separate funds to improve community property**

Suppose that H and W own a house and lot as community property. H uses separate funds of $10,000 to build a swimming pool. The pool takes on the classification of the underlying real property; in this case, community property. The question then is whether reimbursement is appropriate. Prior case law generally held that reimbursement was not appropriate, again using the presumption of a gift.

However under Civil Code § 4800.2, it appears that the spouse using separate funds to improve community property will be entitled to reimbursement. The measure of reimbursement is limited to the amount expended; i.e., it does not include interest or appreciation. Case law suggests that the application of § 4800.2 will be limited to improvements made after January 1, 1984.

G. Personal Injury Awards

The approach taken by the California legislature and courts to the classification of personal injury damages has varied greatly over the years. Theoretically, at least, it would be possible to apportion an award of personal injury damages on the basis of the nature of the compensation; e.g., damages for pain and suffering would be separate property while compensation for lost earnings would be community property. But California has never apportioned personal injury damages in this fashion. California has taken an all or nothing approach. At one time (from 1957–1969), such awards were classified as wholly separate property; at other times they have been classified as community property.

1. **Classification of personal injury awards**

Under the current law, personal injury awards that are recovered during marriage by one spouse from a third person for injuries incurred during marriage are community property.

Example:

Suppose that during marriage, W was driving her car and was rear-ended by another driver. She suffered whiplash injuries and sued the other driver. She recovered $100,000 in damages, or maybe the case was settled, and W received a $100,000 settlement award. The damages or settlement will be classified as community property.

The same classification principle has also been applied to awards similar to personal injury damages, such as workers' compensation awards and disability benefits received during marriage. There are two major exceptions to the classification of personal injury awards as community property:

1) If the cause of action against the third party tortfeasor arose while the spouses were living separate and apart, the recovery will be the separate property of the injured spouse. Suppose in our example that W was living separate and apart from H at the time of the accident. The recovery from the other driver would be W's separate property.

2) The other major exception has to do with the identity of the tortfeasor. If personal injury damages are recovered by one spouse for injuries inflicted by the other spouse, the damages are the separate property of the injured spouse.

There is one more important point to note about personal injury awards. Even where the damages are classified as community property under our basic rule, there are special rules governing the division of community property personal injury damages at dissolution.

2. **Distribution of personal injury awards at dissolution**

On termination of the marriage by dissolution, community property personal injury damages are not subject to the usual equal division requirement. Instead, they are generally assigned to the injured party unless the court determines that "the interests of justice require another disposition." In any event, the injured party must receive at least one-half. This exception to the equal division rule applies only if the personal injury award has not been commingled with other community property. Civil Code § 4800(b)(4).

H. Employment Benefits

1. Retirement Benefits

a. Vested vs. unvested benefits

Prior to *In re Marriage of Brown*, 15 Cal.3d 838 (1976), the California courts distinguished between vested and unvested pension benefits. The courts held that while vested pension or retirement benefits were property rights capable of being classified, valued, and divided at dissolution, unvested rights were in the nature of an expectancy and could not be classified as community property. This distinction was abrogated by the *Brown* decision, so that now all pension rights or retirement benefits, whether vested or unvested, are property within the community property system. To the extent that the benefits stem from employment during marriage, they are classified as community property.

b. **Matured vs. unmatured benefits**

The employee spouse's retirement benefits may be vested after a requisite period of employment, but may not mature until the employee attains a certain retirement age and is eligible to retire. With regard to unmatured benefits that are classified as community property in a dissolution proceedings, the trial court may place a present value on the pension benefits, award the benefits to the employee spouse and award the non-employee spouse other community assets of equal value. Alternatively, the court may continue jurisdiction and award each spouse an appropriate portion of each pension payment as it is paid.

c. **Apportionment of separate and community interests**

The apportionment principles previously considered may also be applicable to retirement benefits in cases where the employee spouse was employed both prior to and during the marriage.

Example:

Suppose that H began to work for ABC Co. prior to marriage. ABC Co. has a pension plan that will enable H to retire after 25 years with retirement benefits of $1,000 per month. H worked for the company for 10 years and then married W. H continued working for the company for another 15 years. Then the couple gets divorced. At issue is the classification of the pension benefits that husband will shortly begin to receive.

In this situation there are two different methods that the court could use in working out an apportionment of the benefits.

(1) **Money contribution method**

One is the money contribution method. The court could look at the amount of contributions made on the husband's behalf to the retirement plan prior to marriage, and the amounts contributed after marriage, and effect an apportionment based on the relative separate property and community contributions to the total contributions.

(2) **The time method**

The other method, probably more commonly used, is the time method. Under the time method, the court would apportion the benefits based on the length of time that the husband worked for ABC prior to marriage and the time worked during marriage.

Example:

H worked a total of 25 years; 10 prior to marriage and 15 during marriage. Therefore, $\frac{10}{25}$ or $\frac{2}{5}$ of the benefits are separate property ($400 per month), and $\frac{15}{25}$ or $\frac{3}{5}$ of the benefits are community property ($600 per month).

2. **Stock options**

Pensions and retirement benefits are not the only form of deferred compensation within the coverage of the community property system. Profit sharing plans and stock option plans have been given similar classification treatment. For example, in *In re Marriage of Hug*, 154 Cal. Ct. App.3d 780, (1984), the court viewed stock options earned during marriage but exercisable after separation as subject to apportionment on a time basis. The employer's motivation in granting the stock options may also be an important factor in classifying them as community or separate property. For example, in *In re Marriage of Harrison*, 179 Cal. Ct. App.3d 1216, (1986), the court concluded that the employer's primary intent was to compensate the employee for future rather than past efforts; the stock options represented "golden handcuffs" to ensure that the employee would stay with the company. This type of factor can be taken into account in working out an appropriate apportionment formula.

3. **Severance pay**

If the termination benefits had been received during marriage and before separation, the benefits would be treated as community property. But where the benefits have been received after separation, the analysis becomes more complex. A significant factor is whether payment of the benefits stemmed from an absolute earned right pursuant to the employment contract. If so, the severance pay is likely to be classified as community property. On the other hand, if the benefits were developed at the time of termination to mitigate the problems accompanying unemployment, they are more likely to be classified as separate property.

4. **Disability payments**

To the extent that disability payments are a substitute for a spouse's earnings during the marriage, they are community property. But post-separation or post-divorce disability payments are ordinarily the disabled spouse's separate property, since they arguably replace post-marriage earnings. However, if a spouse elects to take disability payments (which would be his/her separate property) in lieu of retirement or pension benefits (which are community property), then, subject to the Supremacy Clause, the disability payments are treated as community property to the extent they supplant pension payments.

IV. LIMITATIONS ON CLASSIFICATION

There are certain limitations on the operation of the California community property system. These limitations or restrictions include limitations on property within the community property system, limitation on persons within the community property system, and constitutional limitations.

A. Limitations on Property within the System

Most kinds of legally recognized and protected property interests fit into the community property system without difficulty. However, there are certain relationships of economic value that courts have removed from the system.

1. Professional education

To date, California courts have held that the value of a professional education acquired by a spouse during marriage and the concomitant increased earning capacity are not property within the community property system. It is possible to value a professional education, and it would also be possible to divide that value in some way on dissolution. But California courts have removed this potential asset from the operation of the community property system. The courts' underlying concern seems to be that in valuing and dividing such an asset, reference would have to be made to the post-marital acts of the educated spouse and post-marital acts are not acts for the benefit of the community. The court in *Marriage of Aufmuth*, 89 Cal. Ct. App.3d 446, (1979) stated:

> The value of a legal education lies in the potential for increase in the earning capacity of the acquiring spouse.... A determination that such an asset is community property would require a division of post-dissolution earning to the extent that they are attributable to the law degree, even though such earnings are by definition the separate property of the acquiring spouse.

The legislative response to the professional education problem was the enactment of Civil Code § 4800.3. Under section 4800.3, the value of the professional degree and concomitant enhanced earning capacity is still outside the system, but the community may be entitled to reimbursement for community contributions to the educational costs. The community is generally entitled to reimbursement (plus interest at the legal rate) where community property is used to pay (or satisfy a loan used) for a spouse's education or training, ***provided*** the education or training ***substantially enhanced*** the earning capacity of that spouse; Civil Code § 4800.3. Where this education or training occurred (i) within 10 years of divorce, there is a presumption that the community did ***not*** substantially benefit from it; (ii) if it occurred more than 10 years prior to divorce, there is a presumption that the community ***did*** substantially benefit from it.

It should be noted that unlike a professional education, a professional practice itself is an asset within the system, and is treated like any other business. The professional practice, including any good will component, must be valued and divided at dissolution. The practitioner is generally awarded the practice itself, and the non-practitioner spouse is awarded other community property assets of equal value.

2. **Term Life insurance**

Another asset that may be removed from the operation of the community property system for purposes of division on dissolution is a policy of term life insurance where the insured spouse is still alive. Be careful to distinguish the dissolution from the death situation.

Example:

Suppose that H takes out a policy of term insurance during marriage and pays the quarterly premiums from his earnings during marriage. If H dies during marriage with the policy in force, the proceeds are classified as community property and W has the right to one-half, regardless of who the designated beneficiary is. But where H doesn't die, and H and W get divorced, we have a split of authority as demonstrated in the *Lorenz, Gonzales*, and *Logan* cases.

In re Marriage of Lorenz holds that term insurance has no value while insured is still alive. 146 CA3d 464, 194 CR 237 (1983).

In re Marriage of Gonzales asserts that a term life insurance policy does have economic value and indicates that replacement cost may be used as a valuation method. 168 Cal. Ct. App.3d 1021, (1985).

Estate of Logan holds that term insurance is not divisible as community property, unless the insured becomes uninsurable during the term paid with community funds. 191 Cal. Ct. App.3d 319, (1987).

Note that the above problem arises only with respect to term insurance policies. A ***whole life*** policy, which has cash value, is subject to valuation and division at dissolution.

B. **Constitutional Limitations**

In addition to some judicially imposed restrictions on what is property within the community property system, there are some constitutional limitations on the classification of property as community property.

1. **The Supremacy Clause**

One of the constitutional limitations involves the Supremacy Clause of the U.S. Constitution. As was noted earlier, under the *Brown* decision, retirement benefits, whether vested or unvested, are classifiable as community property. But where retirement or other types of benefits are created by federal legislation, there may be a question of the propriety of classifying them as community property under the California system. The underlying issue is whether the Supremacy Clause of the U.S. Constitution precludes the classification of such benefits as community property. Under the Supremacy Clause, state laws, including state marital property laws, must yield to any conflicting federal law when Congress, in the proper exercise of a constitutionally granted source of power, has expressly or impliedly sought federal supremacy.

The issue of preemption has most frequently arisen in connection with federal statutes establishing military and other types of retirement benefits. California courts repeatedly have held that state community property law was not preempted. But in several United States Supreme Court decisions, preemption has been found.

In *Hisquierdo v. Hisquierdo*, 439 U.S. 572 (1979), the Supreme Court held that a railroad worker's retirement benefits could not be classified and divided as community property. Thus, the husband's benefits were awarded entirely to him. The Supreme Court also indicated that a set-off award of other community property to the wife would not be permissible. In *McCarty v. McCarty*, 453 U.S. 210 (1981), the Supreme Court similarly held that a military retirement pension could not be classified and divided as community property. However, the *McCarty* and *Hisquierdo* holdings have since been abrogated by Congressional legislation, which authorizes a state court to treat railroad and military retirement pay either as separate property or community property in accordance with state law.

Preemption has also been found with respect to other federally created benefits such as the veterans' life insurance program, where the veteran has the absolute right to designate someone other than his spouse as the beneficiary, and the designated beneficiary is entitled to all of the proceeds. The recent United States Supreme Court opinion in *Mansell v. Mansell*, 490 U. S. 581 (1989), holds that military disability pay cannot be classified as community property, even where it operates as a substitute for retirement pay.

If the Bar examination question includes any federally created or federally controlled benefit or property right, the possibility of preemption should be raised and discussed.

2. Due Process and Retroactivity

Another possible constitutional limitation on the operation of California's community property system involves the due process clauses of the state and federal Constitutions, which prohibit the taking of vested property rights without due process of law. The due process issue has arisen primarily in cases involving retroactive application of legislative amendments to the community property system. Early California cases held that statutes that increased the wife's rights in community property could not be applied retroactively so as to impair the vested rights of the husband in property acquired prior to the date of the legislation. This principle of non-retroactivity was initially developed in the case of *Spreckels v. Spreckels*, 116 Cal. 339, 48 P. 228 (1897), which held that an 1891 statute prohibiting the husband from making a gift of community property without his wife's consent could not constitutionally be applied to property acquired before 1891. The *Spreckels* rule was criticized and ultimately rejected by the California Supreme Court in the *Addison* case discussed *infra*, and in *In re Marriage of Bouquet*, 16 Cal.3d 583, 128 CR 427 (1976). In *Bouquet*, the California Supreme Court upheld the retroactive application of the "living separate and apart" statute (Civil Code § 5118) to previously acquired earnings of the husband.

The question of the constitutionality of retroactive application of community property legislation recently arose again in the context of Civil Code §§ 4800.1 and 4800.2. Civil Code §§ 4800.1 and 4800.2 were originally enacted in 1983, and were expressly made applicable to all cases not yet final on January 1, 1984. In 1985 and 1986 the California Supreme Court held that retroactive application of these statutes would be unconstitutional, at least where the cases were filed before January 1, 1984. See *In re Marriage of Buol*, 39 Cal.3d 751 (1985); *In re Marriage of Fabian*, 41 Cal.3d 440 (1986).

In April, 1986 emergency legislation was enacted, changing the effective date to all cases filed after January 1, 1984. This legislation was held unconstitutional in *In re Marriage of Griffius*, 187 CA3d 156 (1986) which indicated that §§ 4800.1 and 4800.2 cannot constitutionally be applied to property acquired prior to January 1, 1984. Thereafter the legislature enacted the current versions of §§ 4800.1 and 4800.2, with an unusual preamble containing public policy declarations and stating that a compelling state interest justifies retroactive application to all cases filed after January 1, 1984. The latest legislation has not yet come before the California Supreme Court, but several Court of Appeal decisions have held that it cannot be constitutionally applied to cases where the property was acquired before January 1, 1984. See, e.g., *In re Marriage of Lockman*, 204 Cal. Ct. App.3d 782 (1988).

There are two major limitations or restrictions on persons coming within the California community property system. The first limitation involves the requisite of a valid marriage; the second is based on the concept of domicile.

1. **Valid Marriage**

   In California, unlike some of the other community property jurisdictions, a valid marriage is prerequisite to the existence of a marital community. Therefore, there can be no community property without a legally binding marriage. The marriage required for the existence of a community in California does not have to be of any special type. It need only be a marriage recognized by the state. Moreover, California recognizes as valid any marriage that is valid under the law of the state where it was contracted.

a. **Putative Spouses**

Suppose that a man and woman go through a marriage ceremony and believe themselves to be legally married, but for one reason or another, the marriage is invalid (either void or voidable).

For example, perhaps the man had been married before, and his divorce from his first wife is not final or is invalid for some reason. Or suppose that the couple live together as husband and wife with an honest belief that common law marriages are valid in California; unknown to them, California does not recognize common law marriages.

To cover these types of situations, commonly called putative marriages, where at least one if not both of the partners has a good faith belief in the existence of a valid marriage, California courts have developed an *equitable* community property system analogous to the legal system. This judicially created equitable community property system recognizes the earnings and accumulations of the putative marriage relationship as equitable community property.

The equitable community property system has now been partially codified at Civil Code § 4452. This provision recognizes the equitable system in dissolution or annulment proceedings; it characterizes the equitable community property as *quasi-marital* property and provides for equal division.

Where the putative marriage relationship is terminated by death, rather than by annulment or dissolution the judicially created equitable community property system will continue to apply.

Following are some examples of the application of the quasi-marital property concept:

(1) **Annulment**

Suppose A and B went through a marriage ceremony and believed that they were validly married. But for one reason or another, the marriage was legally invalid. A and B lived together for 20 years, and accumulated $500,000 worth of property. At this point, their relationship breaks up and annulment proceedings are instituted. Under Civil Code § 4452, the property that would have community property had there been a valid marriage is quasi-marital property and should be divided equally between A and B.

(2) **Guilty Putative Spouse**

Suppose in the preceding example, A was legally married to H at the time of the alleged marriage to B, and A knew she was still married to H. Thus A could not have a good faith belief in the validity of her marriage to B. Suppose that the bulk of the $500,000 accumulated was the result of B's earnings during the putative marriage. Is A still entitled to one-half of the property on termination of the relationship? Or would this be a windfall to a knowing bigamist? Civil Code § 4452, by its terms, indicates that the quasi-marital property system could apply in this situation; however, in the *Marvin* case, the California Supreme Court indicated that the answer is not clear, but did not decide the point.

(3) **Termination by Death: Quasi-Marital Property**

Suppose that A and B lived together as husband and wife with a good faith belief in the existence of a valid marriage and accumulated $500,000 worth of property over their 20-year relationship. Then A dies intestate, survived by B and by her sister S. Assuming that the $500,000 is quasi-marital property, it will be treated like community property for succession purposes, and it will all go to B.

(4) **Termination by Death: Separate Property**

Suppose that in addition to the $500,000 quasi-marital property, A owned 10 shares of stock that she had inherited from her father. Does B get the same intestate share that a surviving spouse would get (i.e., one-half of the decedent's separate property in this situation)?

In *Estate of Leslie*, 37 Cal.3d 186, (1984), the California Supreme Court held that the surviving putative spouse should be treated in the same fashion as a legal spouse for all intestate succession purposes, including succession rights to separate property. It should also be noted that the putative spouse has been accorded the rights of a legal surviving spouse for wrongful death actions, Social Security, and workers' compensation benefit purposes.

(5) **Legal and Putative Spouses**

Suppose H and W married and had a valid marriage. Ten years later, H left W and took up with A. H went through a marriage ceremony with A, but was never divorced from W. H lived with A for 20 years, and then died intestate. During the 20 years that H lived with A, they accumulated $500,000 worth of property.

The question then is what are the rights of W and A with respect to this property? As to W, this property is H's separate property (by virtue of Civil Code § 5118). Under intestacy rules, W is entitled to one-third to one-half. As to A, this property is quasi-marital property, and A would be entitled to it all. The California Court of Appeal faced this problem in *Estate of Hafner*, 184 Cal. Ct. App.3d 1371 (1986).

The court gave one-half to the legal W and decedent's children (of this one-half, one-third to W and two-thirds to decedent's children). The court gave the other half to the putative spouse.

Compare the following example:

> Suppose H and W were validly married, and that shortly after marriage, H took up with another woman, A, and went through a marriage ceremony with her. H kept up two households, spending three days with wife and their children, then four days with A and their children. Neither A nor W knew of the other's existence until H died intestate.

Civil Code § 5118 does not apply here — there has been no separation. There is a legal community living side by side with a putative community. One case dealing with this type of problem used a purely equitable approach and gave one-half of the accumulated property to each "spouse." *Estate of Vargas*, 36 Cal. Ct. App.3d 714 (1974).

But suppose that the husband had left a will, bequeathing all of his property to X; or suppose that the husband did not die, that one of the spouses decided to get divorced, and then discovered the bigamous relationship. No case law exists on this, but various solutions have been suggested:

a. Half to legal community, with quarter going to H and quarter to W; half to putative community, with quarter going to H and quarter to A (But H would end up with more than the innocent parties.)

b. Half to A and half to W

c. A third to each

b. **Non-marital Cohabitation Relationships**

> Suppose A and B lived together, knowing that they were not married to each other. They accumulated property during the period of their cohabitation relationship. They later split up. How should this property be divided?

There is no community property because there is no valid marriage. Nor is there quasi-marital property because neither party had a good faith belief in the existence of a valid marriage. Any rights that each person may have in property acquired by the other must be based on contract. In *Marvin*, the Supreme Court indicated that such a contract could be express, or that it could be implied from the conduct of the parties. The court also indicated that in the absence of an express agreement, the court can fairly divide properly accumulated through mutual effort, in order to protect the parties' lawful expectations. *Marvin v. Marvin*, 18 Cal.3d 660 (1976).

2. Domicile

The second major restriction or limitation on persons within the California community property system involves the concept of domicile.

a. Non-California domiciliaries

The governing principle here is that the marital property rights are controlled by the law of the domicile of the married persons at the time of acquisition. Therefore, if the parties were never domiciled in California then California community property law does not apply, even though the couple may have acquired property here.

Example:

H and W live in Ohio. They decide to take a vacation trip and drive to the West Coast. While in California, W is injured in an automobile accident and sues in California and recovers a $500,000 judgment. The classification of that award is governed by Ohio law, not California law. California courts have applied this principle even where real property was acquired in California by a non-California domiciliary.

b. California Domiciliaries

The converse situation can also arise. Suppose that the husband and wife are California domiciliaries, and that the husband uses his earnings to acquire real property in a non-community property jurisdiction, e.g., Ohio. Some time later, the husband and wife get divorced. Note that the statutory definition of community property at Civil Code § 5110 does not include out-of-state real property. Nevertheless, California courts have classified such real property as community property by using the tracing principle. The real property is traceable back to a moveable asset (i.e., money) acquired during marriage by a California domiciliary.

Note though that under traditional jurisdictional rules the decree of a California court cannot directly affect title to out-of-state real property. The spouse must seek to have the California decree recognized by the courts of the state where the land is located. For this reason, Civil Code § 4800.5 indicates that where possible at dissolution, California courts should award the out-of-state realty to the spouse holding title, and award the other spouse other community property assets of equal value.

To summarize the basic principles thus far: If the parties are California domiciliaries, community property laws will apply, even to out-of-state real property; if the parties are not California domiciliaries, community property laws will not apply, even to California real property.

c. **Parties Changing Domicile**

Suppose H and W married and resided in a common law jurisdiction, e.g., Ohio. They lived there for many years, accumulating substantial property primarily through H's earnings. Eventually H retired, and the couple decided to move to California. They sold their Ohio house, closed out their savings accounts, and came to California. Here they use the sale proceeds from the Ohio house and their savings to buy a small condo and make stock investments. They live off their investments and H's pension. Suppose that a short time later, H dies, or that the couple decides to get divorced. What happens to the condo and the stock?

There is a problem here: If property is classified according to the law of the domicile at the time of acquisition and the tracing principles are applied, we would probably classify all of the items here as husband's separate property under Ohio law. In a common law jurisdiction, even though property is the sole and separate property of the acquiring spouse, the other spouse may be afforded certain statutory protections on death or dissolution. When the couple moves to California those statutory protections are lost. To alleviate this problem, the California legislature developed the concept of quasi-community property. The quasi-community property remedy is generally applicable on termination of the marriage by dissolution or death.

(1) **Quasi-Community Property at Dissolution**

In 1961, the legislature enacted Civil Code § 4803, which provides that all personal and real property, wherever situated and whenever acquired, that would have been community property if acquired by a California domiciliary, will be denominated quasi-community property for purposes of dissolution and will be treated like community property. The constitutionality of this legislation was upheld in *Addison v. Addison*, 62 Cal.2d 558, 399 P.2d 897 (1965).

In *Addison*, the husband and wife were married and resided in Illinois. The husband had accumulated $150,000 worth of personal property with his earnings. The parties later moved to California and the wife filed for divorce in 1961, claiming a right to one-half of the property under the quasi-community property statute. The husband argued that the statute was unconstitutional because it violated the privileges and immunities clause and constituted a taking of his property without due process. The court held that there was no privileges and immunities clause violation, because the statute applies only if a dissolution action is brought after the parties have established a California domicile; the statute is not necessarily connected with a change of domicile at all.

As to the due process challenge, the court acknowledged that there was a taking of husband's property, but indicated that vested property rights may be impaired *with due process.* The state's police power includes the right to interfere with vested property rights whenever reasonably necessary to protect the health, safety, and general welfare. The state has a great interest in controlling marital property rights and protecting its domiciliaries, and in providing an equitable distribution of marital property on dissolution. Therefore the constitutionality of the statute was upheld by the court.

There are certain limitations on the application of Civil Code § 4803. *In re Marriage of Roesch*, 83 Cal. Ct. App.3d 96 (1978), the court held that before a court can apply the quasi-community property statute (1) both husband and wife must be domiciliaries of California and (2) the dissolution action must take place in California. Unless these requisites are met, California does not have a sufficiently strong interest to justify application of its quasi-community property law.

(2) Quasi-Community Property at Death

Similar problems can arise when a married couple moves from a common law jurisdiction to California and the marriage is terminated by death.

Example:

Suppose H and W were married and resided in Ohio. H acquired $500,000 worth of property with his earnings. The couple later moved to California. Then H dies, willing all of his property to son, S, from a former marriage. In the absence of remedial legislation, W would be left with nothing.

To resolve this problem, the legislature enacted California Probate Code §§ 66 and 101–102. These sections provide that all personal property and California real property that would have been community property if acquired by a California domiciliary will be denominated quasi-community property and treated in some ways like community property for intestate and testate succession purposes.

Under these statutes, the husband in the above example has testamentary power only over one-half of the quasi-community property. The surviving spouse (his wife) has a right to the remaining one-half. If the husband had died intestate, the wife would be entitled to all of the quasi-community property.

Suppose that in the preceding example W had died first, and left a will bequeathing all her property to her brother, B. Would B be entitled to one-half of the quasi-community property? The answer is no. The non-acquiring spouse does not have any power of testamentary disposition over the quasi-community property. This is a major distinction between true community property and quasi-community property.

V. MANAGEMENT AND CONTROL

A. General Principles

Until 1951, the husband had the exclusive right to manage and control all of the community property. In 1951, the wife's earnings and personal injury recoveries were put under her control so long as they were kept separate and distinct from other community property and were not invested in real property. Dual management and control ended in 1975, when the legislature instituted the concept of equal management and control. The legislature declared that the equal management and control legislation was to be retroactive; i.e., it would cover property already in existence as well as new acquisitions. Generally speaking, equal management and control means that either spouse has the right to management and control all of the community property.

There are some limited exceptions to the equal management and control principle. One major exception involves a community property business. Under Civil Code § 5125(d), a spouse who is operating or managing a business or an interest in a business which is community personal property has the primary management and control of the business or interest. Another significant exception is a bank account held in the name of one spouse alone. The other spouse does not have management and control rights, even if the account contains community property funds. But with these exceptions, each spouse has equal management and control rights over the community property.

B. Management and Control Restrictions

Management and control rights are not unqualified. There are three important restrictions on management and control:

1) With respect to personal property, neither spouse can make a gift of community personal property or dispose of community personal property without valuable consideration without the written consent of the other spouse.

2) Neither spouse can sell, convey, or encumber the household furniture or the clothing of the other spouse or minor children without the written consent of the other spouse.

3) Neither spouse can convey or encumber community real property even for consideration, unless both spouses join in the conveyance.

These are the major specific restrictions on management and control rights. In addition, there is a general statutory provision that each spouse shall act in good faith with respect to the other spouse in the management and control of the community property.

C. Remedies for Restriction Violations

What happens when one spouse or the other transfers community property in violation of these statutory restrictions? Note that two persons may be in need of protection, depending on the nature of the transaction. In the gift or gratuitous transfer situation, only the spouse needs protection; but where real property has been transferred for consideration, both the spouse and the transferee may be in need of protection.

1. Gifts

Suppose the husband and wife own 100 shares of ABC Co. stock as community property. Either spouse has management and control rights and either could sell the stock, since it is community property. But suppose the husband makes a gift of the stock to his son from a former marriage. The wife does not know of the gift and does not consent. Sometime later the wife learns about it.

The transaction is voidable by the non-consenting spouse, here the wife. If the wife acts during marriage she can have the gift set aside in its entirety, and bring all of the property back into the community. If the wife doesn't learn of the gift until her husband dies, then she can only recapture one-half of the property. The theory here is that the marriage has been terminated by death, and that the injured spouse can trace his or her half interest of the property into the hands of the third person and recapture it as separate property. So the wife could recapture only 50 shares of the stock.

2. Real Property Transfers

Community real property cannot be transferred even for consideration unless both spouses join in the conveyance. Suppose that the husband and wife acquired Blackacre in 1980. Blackacre is community property but title is in the wife's name alone. In 1987, the wife sold Blackacre to X for $50,000. The husband did not join in the conveyance. In 1989, the husband learns of the sale, thinks that his wife was underpaid and wants to set the sale aside. Will the husband be successful? The answer depends on several factors.

Civil Code § 5127 contains a rebuttable presumption of the validity of the transaction. The presumption applies where a spouse who holds record title in his or her name alone transfers community real property to a bona fide purchaser (BFP) for value who has no notice of the marriage. Even if X is such a BFP, the husband may be able to rebut the presumption of validity. If the husband can show that he was not informed about the execution of the instrument and that he did not consent or acquiesce in any way, he may be able to rebut the presumption.

Suppose that X did have notice of the marriage. He cannot rely on the above presumption of validity. But he may be able to prevail if he can establish facts showing that the husband should be estopped to deny the validity of the deal (e.g., if husband participated in negotiations or knew of the transaction and voiced no objection at the time).

Another defense that the husband may have to overcome is the statute of limitations. Civil Code § 5127 contains a one year statute of limitations. The statute begins to run on the date the instrument is recorded. So if X recorded promptly, the husband may be unsuccessful. The one year statute of limitations applies only in favor of a BFP without notice of the marriage relationship.

Suppose that the husband is successful and establishes his right to set the transaction aside. Therefore, the deed by the wife to the purchaser will be effectively voided. What about the $50,000 paid by the purchaser? The courts have held that in this situation, the purchaser is entitled to get his money back.

Note that in this case, the husband acted to avoid the transaction during marriage and under the generally prevailing rule, he would be able to set aside the entire transaction, and recapture all of Blackacre for the community, not just one-half. This rule was affirmed in *Andrade Development Company v. Martin*, 138 Cal. Ct. App.3d 330 (1982). There, the husband contracted to sell community real property to a development company. The wife did not sign the contract. The husband later refused to go through with the sale, and the company sought specific performance, at least as to the husband's one-half. The court held that the entire transaction was voidable, and refused to grant damages or specific performance as to any part of the contract.

Compare *Mitchell v. American Reserve Ins. Co.*, 110 Cal. Ct. App.3d 220 (1980). There the husband encumbered the family residence without his wife's consent. The wife was permitted to set aside only one-half of the encumbrance. The court's reasoning is anomalous; the court indicated that since community property is liable for the husband's debts, the husband should be able to encumber his half of the community property. The court failed to distinguish between secured and unsecured obligations. The case has been criticized and the court in *Andrade* and in several subsequent decisions declined to follow it.

3. **Additional Remedies**

   Civil Code §§ 5125 and 5125.1 recognize a spousal duty to make a full disclosure of community assets and liabilities to the other spouse, the right of a spouse to seek an accounting, and the right to petition the court for access to or use of community property. These rights may be exercised during marriage; a dissolution proceeding is not required to obtain these remedies.

VI. CREDITORS' RIGHTS

A. Basic Principle

Creditors' rights are closely related to management and control principles. With certain limited exceptions, the rights of creditors are generally co-extensive with spousal management and control rights. This means that if the spouse has the right to management and control of the property at issue, his or her creditors can reach that property to satisfy a judgment debt.

Each spouse has the right to manage and control the community property and his or her separate property. The debtor spouse's creditors can usually reach the debtor's separate property and all of the community property. That is the basic rule of thumb, and it covers most cases; however, there are some variations and exceptions.

B. Obligations Arising During Marriage

1. Tort Obligations

A major statutory qualification of the basic creditors' rights principle is seen in the tort judgment situation. The rules governing tort obligations are contained in California Civil Code § 5122. This statute varies in two significant respects from the basic principle concerning creditors' rights:

1) It calls for classification of the tort debt as community or separate; and

2) It provides for preferential access depending on such classification.

If the tort was committed in connection with activities that were primarily for the community's benefit, then the community property is primarily liable, and the tortfeasor's separate property is secondarily liable. On the other hand, if the tort did not arise out of community benefit activities, then the tortfeasor's separate property is primarily liable, and the community property is secondarily liable.

Note that the classification of the tort as community or separate does not really substantively affect the rights of the creditor. It does not increase or decrease the amount of property that the creditor can ultimately reach. So the statute primarily regulates the rights of the spouses vis-a-vis each other.

One problem with the statute is that it offers no definition of community benefit activities. However, it has been suggested that most types of recreational activities would be deemed "community benefit."

2. Contractual Obligations

With respect to contractual obligations incurred during marriage, the basic rule is that the contracting spouse's separate property and the community property are liable.

Thus the only property not liable is the non-contracting spouse's separate property. Even that property may be liable if the contract was for "necessaries." What is a necessary of life depends in part on the standard of living. In one case, a maid employed by wife was held to be a necessary, with the result that husband's separate property was liable for the maid's unpaid wages.

Note that for purposes of creditors' rights, California does not classify contractual obligations as separate or community. However, as between the spouses, the classification of debts may be part of the accounting process at dissolution or death.

Example:

Suppose H owns an apartment building as his separate property. During marriage, he contracted with X to paint and re-roof the building for $5,000. It is not wrongful for H to use community property to pay X's bill. Furthermore, if H did not pay the bill and X sued, X could reach community property to satisfy his judgment. However, if H and W later get divorced, H may have to reimburse the community for those funds.

C. Premarital Obligations

With respect to premarital obligations, under current legislation, the following property is reacheable to satisfy the obligation: The separate property of the debtor, and the community property but not the earnings of the other spouse, so long as the earnings are kept in an account to which the debtor spouse does not have access and are uncommingled with other community property.

VII. DIVISION OF COMMUNITY PROPERTY ON TERMINATION OF THE COMMUNITY

When the marriage relationship is ended by either the death of one spouse or by dissolution, the community ceases to exist, and it is necessary to make a division and distribution of the community property.

A. Dissolution

When a marriage is terminated by dissolution, there are two different ways to achieve a division of the community property. One is through litigation in the context of the dissolution proceeding. The other is by a contract negotiated in connection with the dissolution.

1. Judicial Proceedings: Jurisdiction

Under California Civil Code § 4800, the court has the power to divide the community property and the quasi-community property of the parties in dissolution or legal separation proceedings. This power necessarily includes the power to classify property as separate or community. Once such classification is made, the court has no jurisdiction over the separate property of the parties. However, Civil Code § 4800.4 permits the dissolution court to divide the separate property interests in jointly held property if either party requests a division.

2. The "Equal Division" Requirement

Once the court has classified the community property assets of the parties, it must make an equal division of the community property. (Prior to the enactment of the Family Law Act in 1969, the court could take fault, such as mental cruelty or adultery, into consideration and award the "innocent" spouse a greater portion of the community property. But under the Family Law Act, fault is not an issue, and the community property must be divided equally.)

a. Methods of Division

There are various methods of making a division, and the trial court has a great deal of flexibility in determining which methods are appropriate in a particular case. For example, the court could make a division in kind, awarding one-half to each spouse. So if the community property included 100 shares of ABC stock, the court could award 50 shares to each spouse.

Alternatively the court could award each spouse an undivided one-half interest in the particular asset. Thus, if Blackacre was determined to be community property, the court could award it to husband and wife as tenants in common.

It is also possible for the court to award one spouse certain items, and to award the other spouse other items of equal value. For example, suppose that the family residence and the family business are both community property and each is worth $200,000. The court could award the house to one spouse and the business to the other.

Finally, the court could order a particular asset sold, and the proceeds divided equally between the spouses.

b. Deferred Sale of the Family Residence

Where the only major community property asset is the family residence and the couple has minor children, serious division problems can arise. Suppose that the wife has been awarded custody of the minor children and wants to remain in the family home until the children are grown. A move would be very traumatic to the children who have already been traumatized by the divorce.

There are several options here. One is simply to order the house sold and the proceeds divided equally. Another possibility is for wife to buy out husband's community property interest by using a note. Payments on the note would come from wife's post-separation earnings. This option has been approved by some appellate courts but with reservations, including the fact that the note must be discounted.

Another solution involves the "deferred sale" concept. Under Civil Code § 4700.10, the custodial parent may be awarded temporary exclusive use and possession of the family home during the children's minority. Civil Code

§ 4700.10 enumerates various factors that the trial court must consider in determining where a deferred sale order is appropriate. First the court must determine that a deferred sale is economically feasible; then it must take into account a wide variety of circumstances, including such matters as length of residence, the proximity of the home to schools, and the economic detriment to the non-resident parent. Unless the parties agree otherwise in writing, a deferred sale of family home order may be modified or terminated at any time in the court's discretion.

c. **Out-of-State Real Property**

Suppose the court determines that Whiteacre, located in Oregon, is community property. Title to Whiteacre is in the husband's name alone. California courts cannot directly affect title to out-of-state real property; if the court decreed that the husband and wife have equal interests in Whiteacre, the wife would have to get the decree enforced by the Oregon courts.

To avoid these problems, California Civil Code § 4800.5 states that, if possible, the dissolution court should award Whiteacre to the husband and award the wife other community property assets of equal value. If this is not possible, the court could order the husband to execute a conveyance or could award the wife a money judgment for one-half the value of the out-of-state realty.

d. **Division of Liabilities**

At dissolution, in connection with the division of the community property, the court must also take into consideration the division of liabilities.

For the purposes of dividing liabilities, the court must first categorize the obligations as community or separate, and then assign them pursuant to the provisions of Civil Code §-4800(c). Civil Code § 4800(c) provides for the following allocation of liabilities:

1) Premarital debts shall be confirmed without offset to the spouse who incurred the debt.

2) Debts incurred for community benefit during marriage prior to separation shall be divided equally except where community debts exceed community assets. In the latter event, the court has discretion to assign the debt in an equitable manner, taking into account such factors as the parties' relative abilities to pay.

3) Debts incurred after separation for common necessities of life shall be confirmed to either spouse according to their respective needs and abilities to pay.

4) Debts incurred after separation for non-necessities shall be confirmed without offset to the spouse who incurred the debt.

5) With regard to debts incurred during marriage, the court must classify debts as separate or community. All separate debts shall be confirmed without offset to the spouse who incurred the debt.

3. **Division by Agreement**

Marital Settlement Agreements settlement agreements are probably the most common way of making a property division in connection with a dissolution (these documents terminate the marriage on all fronts and in some portion thereof will contain a section that provides for the division of property). In addition to dividing the couple's property, many agreements also contain provisions for child and spousal support.

4. **Post-Dissolution Remedies**

Suppose that after a dissolution judgment has become final and is no longer appealable, it appears that a significant community asset was concealed by one of the parties or was inadvertently overlooked.

A final dissolution judgment may be set aside only in the event of extrinsic fraud or mistake. Fraud is extrinsic where the defrauded party was deprived of the opportunity to present his or her claim.

B. Death

Turning now to the distribution of community property where the marriage is terminated by death rather than by dissolution.

1. **Testamentary Rights**

Each spouse has full rights of testamentary disposition over his or her separate property and over one-half of the community property. Thus, each spouse is free to will away all of his or her separate property and one-half of the community property to someone other than the surviving spouse.

> **Example:**
>
> Suppose that Blackacre was community property and Whiteacre was H's separate property. H's will left all his property to his son, S. S will get all of Whiteacre and one-half of Blackacre. W owns the other half of Blackacre.

2. **Intestate Succession Rights**

When a spouse dies intestate, the surviving spouse is entitled to all of the community property. The survivor already owns one-half, and receives the other one-half under the intestate succession rules. However, the surviving spouse's rights to the decedent's separate property depend on what other relatives survived the decedent. For example, if the decedent left a spouse and two or more children, the children would receive two-thirds and the spouse would receive one-third of the decedent's separate property.

Because the power of testamentary disposition and the intestate succession rules are different for community property and separate property, classification of property as community property or separate property is frequently an issue in probate proceedings.

VIII. EXAMINATION QUESTION ANALYSIS

A. **Marital status of the parties**

  1. Is there a valid marriage?

  2. Is there a putative marriage?

  3. Is this a non-marital relationship?

B. **Domicile of the parties**

  1. Have the parties always been domiciled in California?

  2. Have the parties never been domiciled in California?

  3. Have the parties moved to California from a non-community property jurisdiction?

C. **Status of property**

  1. Is the interest at issue capable of being valued, classified and divided as community property?

     a. property right vs. mere expectancy

     b. impact of federal law

  2. When was the asset acquired?

     a. pre-marriage or post-separation

     b. during marriage

  3. If acquired during marriage, can the general presumption of community property be rebutted or avoided?

     a. tracing

     b. special presumptions

     c. agreement

D. Nature of relief

1. Are there violations of management and control restrictions?

2. Are third party creditors involved?

3. Does the case involve termination of the community?

    a. dissolution

    b. death

NOTES